At Home
in
The Big Woods

To Rosemary
with best wishes
Nancy Olcott

At Home in the Big Woods

Nancy Overcott

With Illustrations
by Dana Gardner

Taxon Media
Lanesboro, MN

ISBN 1-885209-40-1

_____

Taxon Media is

Eric Thiss, CEO
Dan Beaver, Publisher
Kathie Felix, Editor
Juliet Sloan, Production Assistant

To Martha

Acknowledgements

*For their editing suggestions and encouragement
over the years, I would like to thank
John Torgrimson, editor of the*
Fillmore County Journal *and
Jim Williams, editor of*
Minnesota Birding.

*For their advice and encouragement, I would like to thank
family members and friends, especially
Ann Abrams, Susan Gysland, Mary Lewis,
Marcia Neely and Carol Schumacher.
For his research on local history, I would like to thank
my husband, Art Overcott.*

*Finally, thanks to the people at Zoo Book Sales and
Taxon Media without whom this
book would not be possible:
Eric Thiss, CEO, Dan Beaver, publisher,
and Kathie Felix, editor.*

Contents

Part I

Part II

Introduction

At Home in the Big Woods is a collection of short essays by a
writer with exceptional empathy with wildlife, especially birds, in a
unique setting. The Big Woods is part of an area in southeastern
Minnesota that escaped the last continental glaciation which covered most of the higher latitudes of North America. A limestone
region with a rugged topography unfavorable for agriculture, the
Big Woods supports a rich flora and fauna.

In this unique "Driftless Area," Nancy Overcott and her
husband acquired land and established a homestead where they
have lived for many years. After a brief survey of the region's
flora and fauna, she tells how she fell in love with its birds and
mammals and won their trust. A chickadee alighted on her hand
and a deer approached near enough to be touched. At the right
time of the year, she could step outside her door and see
"yellow-bellied sapsuckers tapping on their favorite elm and
ruby-throated hummingbirds frequenting the same trees for sap
pooling in the woodpecker holes; walk down my driveway and
see waves of migrating warblers, thrushes and sparrows; sit on
the banks of the South Fork of the Root River and watch flocks
of robins, cedar waxwings, golden-crowned kinglets, ruby-
crowned kinglets and yellow-rumped warblers."

Mrs. Overcott's human neighbors are not neglected in her book,
which tells of the odd ways of some of them. Especially exciting is
her account of the elimination of a decaying house by a fire
controlled by the Canton Fire Department, and how they saved an
old spreading oak tree that rose above the flaming building.

Warm attachment to birds and other creatures endears to us the gifted author of this book. Many of the birds mentioned in it are depicted by attractive black-and-white drawings by Dana Gardner, who has illustrated guides to the birds of a number of South and Central American countries. *At Home in the Big Woods* will be enjoyed by readers who love the woods and its inhabitants as its author does.

- Alexander F. Skutch

Nancy Overcott writes about birds and nature. She also writes about people, their history and the many ways that they are connected to the land. Her column, "At Home in the Woods," in the Fillmore County Journal, is written in a simple, poetic style, where finches and white-tailed deer and old farmers and Amish mingle in a world that is both uncomplicated and alive. Nancy Overcott's writing is a soothing balm to our everyday hurried lives.

- John Torgrimson, Publisher,
Fillmore County Journal

Nancy Overcott brings an incredibly perceptive view to her writings on the Big Woods of the Fillmore County area with her insightful essays. Not only is she an excellent naturalist who is sensitive to the diversity of life in the Big Woods, she has also acquired a fascinating "one-hundred year perspective" on the nature and wildlife of Fillmore County. This is because she has also been transcribing the nature journals of Fillmore County country doctor Johan Hvoslef who recorded his own nature notes in that county from about 1880 to 1920. This unique long-term perspective enriches her own writings by instilling a deep appreciation for the history and vulnerability of this area's plant and animal life. It stimulates a concern for preserving Big Woods remnants and captures the essence of natural features and events that we should all take time to seek out and enjoy.

Carrol Henderson, Nongame Wildlife Program Supervisor
Minnesota Department of Natural Resources

Preface

In 1978, my husband and I moved to the Big Woods of Fillmore County in Southeast Minnesota. *At Home in the Big Woods* consists of my essays about the region accompanied by Dana Gardner's black and white drawings. All the people who appear in the essays are real people; some names and details have been changed to protect confidentiality. Many of the essays first appeared in different forms in the *Fillmore County Journal*, or *Minnesota Birding*.

I began to write creatively in 1988 after getting to know the daughter, who I had given up for adoption in 1965. Because we were so much alike and Martha was a writer, I thought maybe I could write too. Before long, I found myself taking a notebook into the woods, sitting on a log and recording my observations and thoughts.

I wrote about the chipmunk scratching in dry leaves and a red-start building a nest. I recorded how it felt to climb into the lime-stone bluffs and find a hollowed out place in the rocks where I could sit listening for coyotes and waiting for my eyes to pick up on faint footprints or little bones. I wrote about my eccentric neigh-bors and the people I met along the township road. I wrote about life and death in the Big Woods; the wonder of new life; the touching moments between parent birds and their young; and the death nature requires to sustain both predators and prey.

Martha supplied the initial impulse for me to write and in subtle ways, like a silent partner, the fact of her existence continues to influence my writing. The woods supplies inspiration and subject matter.

On a hot afternoon in July of 1999, I received a telephone call from Dana Gardner. It took a moment for me to realize that the person calling was the same Dana Gardner as the illustrator of books about birds and natural history. Now living in Berkeley, Dana grew up in the small town of Lanesboro, Minnesota, 14 miles from where I live. He said he had been reading my columns in the *Fillmore County Journal* and would like to illustrate some of them, particularly those about birds.

Dana became interested in art and nature as a child growing up in Lanesboro. Later, while serving in the military in the former Panama Canal Zone, he met the renowned ornithologist and author, Alexander Skutch. After seeing his paintings and drawings, Dr. Skutch invited Dana to visit him on his farm in Costa Rica. Since then, Dana has illustrated many of Dr. Skutch's books on ornithology and natural history. He has also illustrated a number of field guides for the birds of Central and South America and Southeast Asia.

Dana and I met in person for the first time in April 2000 when he came to spend three months in Lanesboro during which time Cornucopia Art Center featured an exhibition of his work. Since our first meeting, we have become good friends. In October 2000, we decided to collaborate on a book.

Our goal has been to provide a book in which the writing is clear and accessible, contains layers of meaning, provokes thought and recognizes both the light and dark sides of life in the Big Woods; to provide accurate drawings that reveal empathy with the subjects and a feel for their particular habitats; to assemble the drawings and essays in a way that is relevant and tells the story of the woods in all its seasons. We hope that my words and Dana's illustrations will bring the reader into an intimate relationship with the wildlife, the bluffs, forests and streams, and the colorful, sometimes eccentric, people that inhabit this beautiful and remote part of Southeast Minnesota.

Nancy Overcott, October, 2002

The Big Woods

In the summer of 1971, my husband and I had just returned to Minneapolis from a year in Tucson, Arizona. We were at a turning point in our lives, but didn't know where to turn. It was the time of flower power, hippies, communes, co-ops, protests and the Vietnam War. Buddhism, sitar music, The Grateful Dead, long hair, bell-bottomed pants, marijuana and LSD were popular. Idealistic young adults were reading *Living the Good Life* by Scott and Helen Nearing, *The Whole Earth Catalog*, Thoreau's *Walden* and books on owner-built homes.

It was my husband's idea to join the back-to-the-land movement, live simply and learn self-sufficiency. In our search for land, we spent six months looking all over the Midwest. Finally, on a cold winter day in January of 1972 in the bluff country of Southeast Minnesota, we found our dream: 62 acres of deciduous woods, hills, limestone bluffs, a perennial stream and springs with water clean enough to drink.

Our property is located in the Big Woods, an area of eastern Fillmore County consisting of small woodlots that were once owned and used by farmers to supply wood for building, heating and cooking. From the 1920s into the 1960s, squatters lived here in small

trailer houses or homemade tarpaper shacks; they supported themselves by hunting, fishing, growing vegetables and working for local
lumbermen. They also produced their own supplies of moonshine.
They never worried about who owned the land and the landowners never bothered them; they were squatting in the back woods
and only the timber had value. Large extended families grew up
here and some folks never left.

In 1972, the Big Woods still retained its Ozarks-like reputation
and was home to certain eccentrics, but no squatters remained.
Because propane and oil had become the fuels of choice, some of
the farmers were selling their woodlots. Otto Schultz and his brother
Walter sold us their 62 acres for $7,500.

Our land has white oak, bur oak and black oak standing ma-
jestically on the upland areas. Black cherry, bitternut hickory and
white ash are also present, along with pasture returning to poplar
and shrubs, including wild plum, black raspberry, gooseberry,
honeysuckle, prickly ash and more. All our slopes and bluffs face
to the north, with elevations between 950 and 1100 feet. On the
slopes, mature American basswood arch their trunks, almost touching their crowns to the ground. Sugar maples abound, some of
them five feet in diameter. Red cedar and ironwood grow throughout the property, as do black walnut and butternut.

In the spring, summer and fall, carpets of wildflowers cover the
ground. The early spring flowers are mostly white and shades of
blue: hepatica, violets, spring-beauties, bloodroot, trout-lilies,
Dutchman's-breeches, rue-anemone and early meadow-rue. Later
come trilliums, Jack-in-the-pulpits, wild geraniums, Canada anemo-
nes, Solomon's-seal and May-apples. In late summer and fall, larger
plants flower in a variety of colors, with yellow most prominent.
Late season flowers include goldenrod, coneflowers, black-eyed
Susans, daisies, yarrow, thistles and jewelweed, a favorite of the
ruby-throated hummingbird.

At the time of purchase, the only access to our property was
off a township road, across a rocky ditch and up a steep tractor
trail leading to a natural clearing where we would build a cabin,
house, workshop and woodshed. Beyond the clearing, the tractor
trail led through the woods and along the drip edge of bluffs down
to the South Fork of the Root River, or Simley Creek, a spring-
fed creek with abundant riffles favored by three species of trout:
native brook, imported rainbow and German brown.

The creek also provides homes for muskrats and beaver and a source of water for white-tailed deer, badgers, mink, opossum, raccoons, woodchucks, gray and red fox, gray and fox squirrels, coyotes, snakes, frogs, lizards, turtles and more than 200 species of birds. Our land borders both sides of the stream for about ¼ mile.

* * *

The Big Woods is part of a geologically unique area, informally called the "Driftless Area," an isolated plateau of sedimentary rock (limestone, dolostone, sandstone and shale) that encompasses parts of southeastern Minnesota, northeastern Iowa, a large part of southwestern Wisconsin and a small corner of northwestern Illinois. This area escaped some or all of the Ice Age glaciations that elsewhere scoured and scraped the top soils, tore up underlying rock, mixed it all together, carried it on with the ice and ultimately deposited it as glacial drift or till when the ice melted.

When the ice fields receded about 12,000 years ago, they left behind Lake Agassiz, a huge pool of melt water that covered much of northwestern Minnesota and adjoining parts of Canada. The lake eventually broke through its banks and its torrent of floodwater helped to create the region we know today as bluff country. The resulting rivers and streams continue to carve this landscape.

Big Woods Trailer

Changes also continue to occur below the surface. As precipitation and ground water move across and through the carbonate (limestone and dolostone) bedrock, the rock slowly dissolves, eventually leading to sinkholes, blind valleys, caves, disappearing streams and springs, all characteristics of karst topography. Karst terrain has distinctive characteristics of relief and drainage, arising primarily from the chemical process of dissolution, with surface effects playing an important secondary role. Fillmore County is known as the karst capitol of the Upper Mississippi Valley.

Due to its geological makeup and position at a juncture where climatic forces have for millennia shifted across central North America, Southeast Minnesota is the most biologically diverse area in the state. It covers only three percent of the state and contains

May-Apple

30 distinct habitat types and 43 of Minnesota's rare plants, birds, amphibians and reptiles.

Fillmore is the most biologically diverse county within this area. Here can be found lowland hardwood forests, dry prairies, wet meadows and other plant communities containing some of the state's rarest plant species, including Iowa golden saxifrage, narrow-leaved vervain and false mermaid.

However, due to farming, logging and population pressures, few intact natural communities remain. Most are along river bluffs and streams, such as Wisel Creek, Shattuck Creek, Spring Valley Creek, Bear Creek, Diamond Creek and the South Fork of the Root River.

Forestville State Park contains the largest area of continuous habitat in the county and the county's largest concentration of rare birds, including the cerulean warbler, Acadian flycatcher, and Louisiana waterthrush. It is also home to rare snakes, including the racer, the gopher, and the timber rattler.

Because of its rare algific slopes and maderate cliffs, Forestville is one of the most biologically significant spots in the county. These slopes and cliffs are areas in which chilled air from underground ice caves creates cold microclimates for plant species uncommon in Southeast Minnesota, such as mountain maple and yellow birch. Here, in mid-summer, vapor comes from cracks in the rocks and you can reach in and actually touch ice.

Although a growing number of people wish to preserve these habitats through sustainable agricultural and economic development, logging, urban sprawl and certain farming practices, such as large feedlot operations have left their mark. Logging pressures in the Big Woods have increased the number of forest edges, making it difficult for woodland birds to find suitable places to nest. This makes it easy for the edge-loving parasitic brown-headed cowbird to place its own eggs in other birds' nests, increasing its population at the expense of its hosts.

Although Fillmore County experiences some pressure for housing and development, its population remains at a low 23,000. The residents live on farms, in the woodlands and in small towns. The county has one traffic light and 14 incorporated towns, ranging in population from 94 to 2,461 residents.

Our address is Canton, a town 10 miles from our land, with a population of 362. Other towns within a 15-20 mile radius of us are: Preston, the county seat (population 1,530); Harmony (population 1,081); Mabel (population 745); Lanesboro (population 858) and Rushford (population 1,485).

We are surrounded by the smaller unincorporated towns of Lenora and Newburg, both of which have historical churches; Tawney; Chicken Town; Whalen; Prosper, seven miles south of us on the Iowa border; Amherst, which still has an operating country store; Highland, which also has a store; and Henrytown, where a strawberry festival is held every year.

The predominant nationality is Norwegian. Most of the inhabitants have slight Norwegian accents; a few have strong accents, although they have never been to Norway. A native is someone whose family has lived here for more than one generation. Each town still has its unique set of surnames.

* * *

Every relationship and encounter in this rural area must be brought to a personal level, the only level where comfort exists. This need for personal identity is clear in the common question "Who are *you*, then?"

A newcomer soon learns what to expect when she meets a person who doesn't know her. The person never introduces herself, but immediately asks, "Who are *you*, then?" When the newcomer answers, the questioner always looks quizzically and says, "Never heard that name before." The next question is, "Where do you live, then?" and the newcomer must offer the name of someone familiar who lives near her or the questions will continue.

Everyone has a place here, even the alcoholic, schizophrenic and recluse. The important thing is to fit somewhere. Most of our fellow citizens know where we live now; they can physically place us in the Big Woods and they can fit our personal characteristics into certain niches. They know me as a writer for the *Fillmore County Journal*, the Bird Lady and nurse at Green Lea Manor. They know my husband for his map-making, furniture building and his fierce protection of the woods and its creatures.

Although we have retained some of our big city thinking, we have changed to fit our rural community. We have learned to beat around the bush, to come to the point only indirectly and only after engaging in the requisite amount of small talk, including an occasional "uff-dah." We have also learned the waves:

single-finger-lifted-off-the-steering-wheel, a slight raising of the chin and the full five-fingered wave.

In the 30 years since we bought our land, the Big Woods has changed and, in some ways, has remained the same. Most of the old people we knew when we came here are gone. More people like us have moved here to escape the rat race of the city. Small parcels of land are still common, often with absentee owners from urban areas who come here only for weekends and vacations. Many of the big trees have been cut for lumber. Many still stand.

Like the trees, we have put our roots deep into this earth. Although we belong to the human culture here, our best fit is with the Big Woods itself, which seems to contain us in its identity.

Nodding Trillium

Rueben

In May 1972, we packed blueprints, windows, a saw, hammers, nails, our cat and ourselves into our Volkswagen beetle and left Minneapolis to build a cabin on our land. In Prosper, Minnesota, we found a lumberyard that would pre-cut and deliver all of the lumber for the framing of our cabin. We also bought plywood, cement blocks and string. In Burr Oak, Iowa, we bought a used door. Then we began to measure, dig, saw and hammer. Soon we had company.

An old man emerged from the woods, walking stick in hand. "I heard you hammering," he said with a Norwegian accent. "Who are you, then?" When we told him our last name, he slowly shook his head. "Never heard that name before. It's not Norwegian. Where are you from, then?"

"Minneapolis."

"What did you pay for the land?"

"Seventy-five hundred."

He slowly shook his head. "Too much for rough land." An hour later, our visitor picked up his walking stick again.

"What's your name?" we asked.

"Rueben Blagsvedt. I'm your neighbor down the hill. You can come on down anytime you want."

Our idealism and plans for a utopian return to nature were unshakable. We hoped to move to our land permanently in a few years. In the meantime, my husband Art made furniture and I sewed clothes, crocheted blankets and baked bread and cookies. We bought our food out of big drums at the North Country Co-op in Minneapolis where we also bought a Humble wood heater and books to help us become self-sufficient on our land.

On my first visit to Rueben, I brought some of my homemade bread. He lived in a ramshackle wood frame house attached to an old log cabin down by the South Fork of the Root River. He drew water from a spring and had no need for electricity.

On my second visit, I saw another man standing in Rueben's doorway, a tall thin person with long disheveled hair, a scraggly

Rueben's House

beard and a shotgun over his shoulder. When I approached the door, he spit out a wad of tobacco and said, "Paid too much for those woodlots."

The man was Leland, Rueben's son, also known as Pancake. While we talked, I tried not to look too hard at the dead kitten draped over a fence or the dead dog still chained to his doghouse. Sheep grazed in the yard and adjacent field. The voice of Garner Ted Armstrong came from a battery-operated radio. Rueben, who was sitting on a wooden chair just outside his house, invited me in. When I walked through the door, he proudly pointed to a huge wasp nest hanging over the doorway. The wasps were flying in and out of the house.

Rueben began to heat water on a wood stove, pushed away clutter on the kitchen table and offered me some Oreo cookies. Then he offered me coffee. I delivered my homemade oatmeal cookies, which he carefully put away in a cupboard. When I was ready to leave, he told me to walk home along the road, that it might not be safe walking through the woods.

* * *

By the middle of June, we had a roof over our heads and could sleep in our cabin, instead of the Volkswagen. The cabin measured 12 x 12 feet. We had one window in each of three walls and a door in the fourth. A loft held our mattress and provided a small amount of storage space. A ladder led up to the loft. We had to crawl onto our mattress; there was no room to sit or stand.

Against the walls below were shelves, a table, cupboards and a counter where we kept our Coleman stove. A small wood heater sat in one corner. We felt proud that we had built the cabin without the use of electricity.

* * *

One day, as we finished supper, we looked up to find two mules pulling a covered wagon up our driveway. This was our first meeting with our neighbors, Phyllis and Bobby Norby.

"Got to get a culvert at the bottom of your driveway," Bobby said. "You're gonna go right off the edge someday. The township has to put it in for you. You need to talk to Clarence Hegna, the township supervisor; he lives up there on the hill.

"We live over there, about a mile from you, where the dirt road leads down to the Wisel. Used to be a little town there. All's left is an old barn and a cemetery.

"I raised these mules from babies. Aren't they beauts? Stronger than a tractor. Thought we'd take you for a ride."

We climbed into the wagon and drove down the old tractor trail. When we arrived at a big maple tree, Phyllis told us about Rueben's wife, Lija.

"Lija used to wander all over the woods. You never knew when she'd show up at your house. Always thought someone was out to get her.

"One day she had it in mind to go to Amherst for ice cream. Rueben said they had to do the milking first, but Lija wouldn't wait. She took her purse and started walking through the woods.

"They found her frozen to death a day later, right here under this tree, purse in hand, with her little dog barking at her side."

We crossed the boundary of our land and turned toward the South Fork on a steep rocky trail. I tried to look nonchalant while holding on to the wagon for dear life. Here were the bluffs I would come to know well and the creek where I would wander and find the peace I badly needed.

"There's timber rattlers up in these hills," said Bobby. "Got to watch where you're going. I hunt them. Bring a good bounty. Have better luck over by Choice, by the South Fork Church. There's bear around here, too. They just saw one over by Yucatan."

The mules pulled us back into the bluffs the same way we had come down. When we reached our cabin, we thanked the Norbys for the ride and watched them disappear down our driveway in their covered wagon.

We soon learned more about the Norbys. They weren't alone up on their hill; one daughter lived with them in their mobile home and two sons lived nearby with their wives and children. Phyllis raised chickens and planted a huge garden. Bobby raised pigs, horses and mules and planted a potato patch down by the Wisel. He and his sons ran a sawmill.

* * *

We decided to plant a small garden beside our cabin.

Barred Owl

"Those tomatoes will never grow," said Rueben. "Don't have enough sun under that big old oak."

Sun or not, the tomatoes grew and we had cucumbers bigger than we'd ever seen. We decided that, when we finally moved to

Author's Cabin and Deer

our land, we'd have a big garden and maybe raise some chickens and pigs ourselves.

* * *

One weekend when we visited our woods, we discovered a bulldozer on our land and a dirt road from the edge of the tractor path, which had become our driveway, through the woods to a partially cleared field bordering our property. The dozer owner didn't show up all weekend, so we left a note on his machine saying, "Keep your bulldozer off our land!"

The next weekend, a pickup truck arrived at our cabin. A heavy-set man got out and pounded on our door. It was the bulldozer man. He began to yell at us, saying he needed to cross our property to get to his field and, if we wouldn't let him, he wouldn't allow us to use our driveway, which cut across a small corner of his property.

Art told him we wouldn't tolerate his machinery on our land, regardless of his threats. The man, Darrell Nordstrom, turned around, got into his truck, slammed the door and drove away. It didn't take long for me to realize this was a male territorial challenge that I could neither understand nor solve.

We went directly to Rueben for advice.

"You need to talk to Clarence Hegna," he said, "the township supervisor. I'll go with you."

When the three of us arrived at Hegna's, Rueben introduced us to Clarence and his wife, who already knew about us. They invited us in for coffee and brownies.

We let Rueben take the lead and the conversation turned to the weather, neighborhood news and local politics. When Rueben finally described our dilemma, casually inserting it into the stream of conversation, Clarence thought for a while, then slowly said, "Darrell has a tendency to get worked up. I'll talk to him about it."

Clarence also told us we could continue to use our driveway, since it had been the customary access to our land for many years.

Our border war was over. We heard nothing more from Darrell. When the township finally decided to install a culvert at the entrance to our driveway, the entrance was moved so that it was completely on our land. Darrell was the man the township hired to do the bulldozer work.

Fall came. Whenever we visited the woods, I stopped to see Rueben and Pancake. Just before winter started, I knitted hats, mittens and an afghan for them. I don't think they ever used my gifts, just put them carefully away in a drawer.

Winter didn't keep us away from our land, although we had to park our new Chevy pickup at the bottom of the driveway. We couldn't drive it up in the snow. We chopped wood for our wood heater and hauled water in jugs from our spring down by the road.

At night, we heard coyotes howl and the hooting of barred owls. One night we heard a knock and a scratching on our cabin door. We were startled and a little afraid, but it was only Pancake and his dog. We invited them in.

We offered Pancake a beer and he drank our entire supply. Every once in a while he stepped outside to spit and pee. In the morning, we found patches of yellow in the snow all around the cabin and Pancake's footprints weaving through the woods.

One day, Pancake showed us the log cabin he had built on a hill overlooking the valley. Hanging in front of his cabin were the pelts of creatures he had hunted and trapped. He also showed us his collection of Indian artifacts. His greatest treasure was an intact peace pipe.

"Used to be an Indian encampment right here on the creek," he said, "but I find the best stuff over by Yucatan. I'll take you there someday."

And he did. We scrounged around with him in woods and corn-fields. He looked at every artifact we thought we'd found and slowly shook his head.

"Nope. Just a rock," he said.

* * *

In 1978, we finally left the city for good. We had electricity and a well, had paid for our land and had built ourselves a house. Our first year, we planted a huge garden and built a woodshed and a workshop. But, we didn't succeed in becoming self-suffi-cient.

After two years, including one particularly hard winter, we decided to move temporarily to Rochester, 50 miles north of our land, where Art would work to put me through nursing school.

During the four years we lived in Rochester, we visited our

land off and on. I continued to visit Rueben, although Pancake had grown distant. He was drinking more and sometimes he frightened me.

One summer day, just as we arrived in the woods, the Norbys came to tell us Rueben was in the hospital with cancer and Pancake had died in a car accident. Our country roads can be treacherous at night, especially if a driver is as drunk as Leland was when he hit another car, killing the driver and her child, along with himself.

The next time we visited our land, we went to check on Rueben and found him sitting in his log cabin peeling potatoes next to an oil-burning stove. Wasps were flying around the potatoes. A barn swallow flew in the open door and out a broken window.

Rueben said, "I was always afraid Leland would get into trouble and hurt somebody. Now I can die without worrying about him."

That was the last time we saw Rueben alive. I miss him. I have forgotten his face now, but I can still see clearly an old man emerging from the woods, walking stick in hand.

Lilly

On the edge of the Big Woods, five miles from our land by road (three as the crow flies) is the village of Amherst, which dates back to 1853. Because its pioneer settlers built houses strung out along the road, the village was first called Strung Out Town, later shortened to String Town. Eventually, E.P. Eddy, one of the area's pioneers, named it Amherst, in honor of his wife's home town of Amherst, Ohio. Over the years, the town has shrunk to three houses, the skeleton of a one-room schoolhouse and a country store. The post office closed in 1902.

Art and I visited the Amherst store for the first time in 1972. We had come to buy bread, cigarettes and gas. Lilly Haagenson, the proprietor, already knew something about us.

She spoke loudly as though calling from a long distance, "Are you the city people building a house over there in the woods? I wouldn't want to live there. Too lonely for me."

Lilly was a small woman in her late fifties whose craggy face made her look older than she was.

The store was a wood frame building that had been a creamery and sometime dance hall. It wasn't recognizable as a store, except for two clues: a single gas pump in front of the building and a small Wonder Bread sign on the door.

Inside, to the left of the door, was a glass case of refrigerated goods containing bologna, cheese, whole milk and locally-produced Spring Grove soda. Just beyond the refrigerated goods, a cash register sat on a counter. Behind the counter, two shelves held cigarettes, tobacco and candy. Underneath the shelves stood a freezer full of ice cream. To the right were three shelves partially filled with white enriched Wonder Bread, dusty canned goods, crackers, cookies and potato chips.

At the back of the store, we saw a large kerosene heater, a beige couch and a couple of overstuffed chairs with the stuffing coming out. Five men in overalls, with seed caps on their heads, occupied the chairs and couch.

Someone we'd never met said to us: "Heard you went in the ditch with that new Chevy pickup. You've got to get a culvert. Township has to put it in for you."

We hoped for introductions as we chatted with Lilly and the men, but none were offered.

Finally, we took our single loaf of Wonder Bread to the counter and asked for a pack of Winston cigarettes. We knew better than to take more than one loaf of bread. Word had it that Lilly would only sell one loaf to a customer because she always saved some for her other customers.

When we asked for gas, Lilly said, "Can't fill you up today. Getting low on gas. Have to save some for the farmers."

In the years following our first visit, we often purchased supplies at the Amherst store. As time went by, we stopped there less frequently. One day after a long absence, I stopped in for some ice cream. By then I had become a registered nurse and was working in a cancer unit at Methodist Hospital in Rochester.

When I walked in the door, the first thing Lilly said to me was, "I heard you took good care of Mrs. Jorgenson when she was up there dying of cancer. She never had a chance, poor woman. They opened her up, took one look and sewed her right back up again."

Later, when I began to work at the nursing home in Mabel, Lilly asked me about her friend Lucy Johnson, a resident in the home. Lucy had been the proprietor of the Tawney store, about 10 miles from Amherst, for many years. At this point, all that remained of the town of Tawney was a historical marker.

After another long absence, I visited Lilly's store with two California friends. As we drove up and parked in front, Lilly came out of her house on the hill and slowly made her way down to meet us. To me, she looked smaller and frailer than she had before, but her demeanor was as crotchety as ever and her face looked the same as always.

She spoke loudly, as though calling from a long distance. "It's hard for me to get around anymore. My back is so bad you know. I'm 85 now and I've been running this store since 1954."

At first, I didn't think Lilly remembered me. Then she talked about some of the residents in the nursing home and asked if I wasn't lonely "living over there in the woods."

When I introduced her to my friends, she kept right on talking about local people and events, as though we all knew what she was talking about. She mentioned her hair several times. She was worried that the set was going out. She said her son had given her the money to have her hair done for her birthday the week before. Because it cost so much, she wanted to keep it nice for a while yet. Finally, we bought our snacks and left.

My friends were so taken with Lilly that I began to see her through different eyes. I saw her as the treasure she is—a person from a different time, before the days of spin, someone who makes no excuses, who is exactly who she is.

Amherst Store

The House

In 1976, before we had electricity or a well, we began to build a small house—24 x 36 feet—that would sit on 16 treated posts. One Saturday in June, we measured the layout of the posts and started breaking ground. By the end of the day, we had completed work on 10 posts. We were stiff from digging up rocks, carrying cement blocks and holding the posthole digger, which shook like a jackhammer. We were tired and satisfied with our accomplishments.

Our goal for the next day was to finish the posts before returning to Minneapolis and our weekday jobs. Rain poured down. Every step we took made a sucking sound as we dragged our feet up out of the mud. We reached our goal, in spite of the weather. At day's end, though, our house site was ugly and muddy. We had marred the woods in a way the birds that nest here could never do.

After completing the foundation, we moved along at a good pace. We built a double floor with a thick bed of insulation sandwiched between the two layers. We framed the walls on the flat surface of the floor. We lifted one whole wall at a time; I held the wall steady while Art nailed the sill to the floor.

The rafters were difficult to put in place. After trying several methods, we settled on using a rope as a pulley, with Art sitting on the plate (top) of a wall and me pulling on the rope while standing on the floor. Slowly the rafters rose. Art guided them into place. One rafter fell and we had to reconstruct it. Finally, we had the full skeleton of a house.

We managed the siding with me holding the 4 x 8-foot sheets of plywood while Art nailed them to the frame. Art's brother, Jim, and his son, Bill, helped us pull sheets of plywood up to the roof and tack them in place.

* * *

One day, when we were on the roof nailing, the four Amherst Township supervisors paid us a visit to discuss the installation of a culvert at the entrance to our driveway. If they hadn't seen us working so diligently (and with our house so far along), it might have taken longer to convince them that we would become permanent residents of the Big Woods and citizens worthy of a culvert.

Tri-County Electric also visited us and finally provided electricity. Soon after that, we called Larson Well Drilling to dig our well and asked Stanley Hongerholt to come with his bulldozer and grade the old tractor path into a real driveway.

The roof shingling was my job and I didn't do it quite straight. It was the first thing my dad, a woodworking teacher, noticed when he came to visit. When he learned I was the roofer, he wasn't as critical as he might have been.

Little by little, our house became livable, although my dad would always call it a cabin. We had an open design with vaulted ceilings. The house would never be quite complete; over the years, we would modify it to meet our changing needs and tastes. It would grow with us like the shell on a turtle's back.

In 1978, when we moved to our land from Minneapolis, we built a workshop for Art's woodworking tools. Soon after that, Art made and installed molding in the house and added a wall with an arched opening between the kitchen and living room. He built bookshelves across one entire living room wall and two floor-to-ceiling paned windows.

We added a roofed porch to the south side of the house, overlooking our huge garden. We would eventually fence this porch with chicken wire for our Siamese cats, Izzy and Sarah, and all the cats that would follow them, so they could be outside without threatening the birds and small mammals.

By 1980, we were tired of all the work—planting and harvesting the huge garden, putting food by, cutting and hauling firewood, trying to keep two old cars running and trying to keep our driveway passable in the winter. I was working full time at the Mabel Bank while Art worked on finishing the house. We were both crabby and our marriage was in trouble. It was then that we decided to move to Rochester where I would attend nursing school.

In that same year, Art and I began to search for the baby we had given up for adoption in 1965. We followed a trail of information and found her 9th grade picture in a school yearbook. She was living in Rochester with her adopted family. We did not try to

Cat by Wood Stove

contact her. It was enough just to have a picture and know that she was alive.

In 1982, I started working as an R.N. on the night shift at Rochester Methodist Hospital. Friends of friends moved into our house in the woods. They lived there rent-free and their presence protected the house from vandals.

For a while we thought of moving to California, but finally decided to give the woods another try. In the spring of 1984, we drew up plans for an addition to the house. At first, we thought a simple bay window addition would be nice, but our plans grew and evolved into a 16 x 36-foot structure consisting of two rooms, a storeroom, a hallway and a porch. One of the rooms would be Art's study and one would be my sunroom and study. The porch facing into the woods would house my muse.

We asked the couple living in our house to move out. Art moved in and began the addition. I remained in our Rochester apartment and continued to work the night shift at Methodist Hospital.

During this period, I received frequent panicky calls from my dad who was doing his best to care for my mom, who was dying of breast cancer. Mom had struggled with this illness for 16 years before she refused further treatment, saying she was ready to die.

On one of my many trips to Faribault to help care for her, Mom talked for the first time about my out-of-wedlock pregnancy and the baby I had given up for adoption. She said she was sorry she hadn't encouraged me to keep the baby.

On my last trip to care for my mom, I could see it was time. She died in my arms the day after I arrived. It was a relief to know that she wasn't suffering any more, but it was almost impossible to comprehend that she no longer existed.

At first, Dad and I were busy making arrangements for the funeral and receiving guests who came to offer sympathy. Grieving would come later. My sister Ann wasn't able to attend the funeral; she was in poor health and couldn't make the trip from Tucson. Instead, we spent hours talking with each other on the phone.

After Mom's funeral, the anxious calls from my dad increased in frequency. He was lost without his wife of 44 years. I felt a little panicky myself when he began calling me by my mother's name. I knew I wasn't as strong as she had been, but it looked as if I would have to take her place in caring for my dad.

A couple of months after my mom's death, I started working

the evening shift at the hospital and moved back to the Big Woods. I planned to commute the 50 miles each way to work.

* * *

By the end of August, Art had completed the shell of our addition. During that time, he was also helping to build the house of our neighbors, Kathy and Erik Erickson, who had just moved to the Big Woods from Burnsville, a suburb of Minneapolis.

Meanwhile, I had been hacking my way through the woods, cutting trails with a hatchet and pruning shears. I cut down prickly ash and honeysuckle and trimmed the tarantula-like stalks of gooseberry bushes. I followed animal trails when I could find them, then later found the animals following my trails. Art built wooden benches to place along the trails.

In December, my dad had a heart attack and bypass surgery.

In the spring of 1985, Dad had gallbladder surgery. While taking care of him in Faribault, I learned that Martha, the daughter Art and I had given up for adoption, wanted to meet us. We met her and her parents at the Children's Home Society in St. Paul. We didn't hear from her again for two and a half years. Our hearts were raw.

After too many years of living on plywood floors, we finally installed wood floors in the living room, hallway and my sunroom. We put linoleum on the kitchen floor and carpeting in the bedroom and Art's study. We also lowered the ceiling in the bedroom.

In 1988, Martha began to weave in and out of our lives. Our meetings were as awkward as they were intimate. We were strangers who were not strangers. We recognized the same character traits in each other, especially the intensity and sensitivity.

All three of us were serious readers. Martha and I liked the same authors. Martha was an aspiring writer. She gave me some of her essays and journals to read. She has a sparse, clear style that intimates more than it explains. It shows her quirky sense of humor and reveals her willingness to confront the dark side of life.

I thought that, if she could write, maybe I could too. I began to write about her. After a while, I found it more rewarding and less fraught with emotion to write about the woods, other people and birds.

And yet, something about Martha or my experience of her always appears in my writing—in the way I write about the woods, new life in the spring, parent birds and their anxiety for their young, death and loss. Writing connects me to Martha; it is my way of never losing her.

In the spring of 1990, I left my job in Rochester to work at Green Lea Manor in Mabel, only 14 miles away. Art and Andrea, his daughter from a long-ago marriage, became reacquainted. Andrea became a welcome part of our lives. She and Martha met for the first time. They didn't seem like sisters and showed no signs of becoming close.

On October 13, 1990, I received another of those panicky calls from my dad. He said he was going to shoot himself and that he wanted me "to come and pick up the pieces." I told him that I didn't believe him. Five minutes after we hung up, I received a call from his neighbor. He had indeed shot himself. He had used his favorite hunting gun. I was numb.

As we drove to Faribault, I felt a strange giddiness. My adrenaline was pumping. I also felt fearful, angry, guilty and sad.

I became obsessed with reaching my sister. I knew she wouldn't be able to make the trip from Tucson; her health was continuing to deteriorate. When I finally reached her, her reaction was, "How could he do this to us?"

I got through those first days by writing about my dad. I still write about him from time to time. Exhibiting the same perfectionism he had exhibited all his life, I made funeral arrangements, contacted relatives and began to go through all my parents' stuff. It took a year to sort through everything, sell the house and complete all the documents for the estate.

From Dad's house, I brought home some of the furniture he had built: a walnut desk, a cherry side table, an inlaid mahogany end table and a walnut wastebasket. I kept some of Mom's things as well: her Sterling silver, Spode china, crystalware, jewelry and needlework. With part of my inheritance, we bought a new Ford tractor with a plow.

In 1994, we bought a sailboat and began sailing on Lake Pepin, a wide part of the Mississippi River 90 miles northeast of our land. Art's daughter, Andrea, often sailed with us.

In 1995, we added a porch to the front of our house. A few years later, because it didn't have a roof, it began to rot. In 2000, Art demolished the porch. The next spring we built another larger porch; this time with a roof, so that it wouldn't rot.

The Workshop

In 1997, a big wind blew some shingles off the roof of our workshop. We patched the resulting leaks, thinking we would soon return to make permanent repairs. As time went by, various excuses kept us from starting what we knew would mean re-roofing the entire shop and reclaiming our water-damaged possessions. In the meantime, our patches failed and we pushed the problem to the back of our minds.

Who knows what makes a person finally decide to remedy a situation that has deteriorated during years of procrastination? One day, in 2000, I found myself standing on the roof of our workshop assisting Art as he hammered nails into new metal roofing.

I held one end of a rope; Art had tied the opposite end around his waist, in the hope that I could prevent him from sliding off the slippery metal. Although alert to the danger my husband was facing, I didn't have much to do and my attention wandered.

I noticed the wren Art calls friend, carrying food to her nestlings somewhere inside the shop. A red-eyed vireo jabbed food down the gaping mouths of her offspring. A robin fed a fledgling. The phoebe, with food in her mouth, flew to her nest in a canoe stored under the eves of the shop. We weren't the only ones working in the woods.

This bird's eye view gave me a new perspective on the work necessary to support our lifestyle. It was hard to believe the two of us alone had built this shop, which measured 24 x 36 feet with a 56 x 36-foot overhanging roof. Of course, we did it more than 20 years ago—when we felt about a century younger.

But, even so, how did we manage to staple all the insulation between the studs of that high open ceiling? How did we muscle the rafters up? And where did we get the energy and strength to cut our own wood for the framing?

These thoughts took me back to the spring of 1978. We had learned that we were not the only idealistic members of the back-to-the-land movement in Fillmore County. Living near us in an owner-built log cabin, Mary Lewis and Phil Rutter were planting American chestnut trees for what would become the Badgersett

Northern Bobwhite

Research Farm. They introduced us to Steve and Janene Roessler, who lived in an owner-built combination workshop and house in the woods near Preston.

The two couples asked if we wanted to join them in thinning some red pines near Rushford. The lumber we cut would be our payment. We agreed to join the project; the pine logs would be perfect for the framing for our workshop. Soon, a summertime odyssey began, during which the six of us achieved the kind of intimacy similar to that of our Amish neighbors, an intimacy that came from shared ideals and physical labor.

Steve and Janene volunteered their truck, which was large enough to haul wagonloads of logs. Their neighbors, who owned the farm and cathedral of a barn that eventually became the Old Barn Resort, loaned us a wagon.

Our days went something like this: We would meet at the old barn prepared with chainsaws, chainsaw paraphernalia, crowbars, water, Mary's peanut butter cookies and all the strength our healthy young bodies could muster. When we reached the pines, we would decide which trees to cut and the direction we wanted them to fall.

Each tree would be felled by cutting a wedge near its base, then cutting straight through from the opposite side. When a tree was down, the men would cut off the branches and the women would haul the branches away. Most of the logs were more than 15 feet long and it sometimes took all six of us to carry a single log to the wagon.

During our breaks, we would sit on a log, drinking water, eating cookies and talking about our decisions to move to the country, how we each found our particular dream property and the books that influenced us.

Our reverence for the earth bordered on the religious and we talked about ways to preserve our planet. Mary and Phil had solar power and a windmill. Steve and Janene had plans for an earth-sheltered home. Art and I had built an efficient small house and used electricity sparingly. We all planted huge gardens, gathered wild berries and put food by.

We also talked about ways to make a living: planting and selling trees, making furniture, building houses, selling or trading produce and, like the Amish, working for each other. As a group, we had raised a shed on Rutter's property, shingled the roof of our workshop and carried rocks for a wall at Roessler's.

One option we didn't like to talk about was working away from home. To my surprise, I was the first of us to work at a conventional job.

Whenever we heard a bobwhite calling, our conversation would stop abruptly. We had all heard bobwhites near our homes, but not often, so the sound was always a treat. We had no idea how difficult it would become to find or hear this bird only a few years later.

We would usually do two loads of logs and would stay for dinner at whoever's house we ended the day.

Our life was not all work. We learned to play together, too—having dinner parties, attending area dances, bluegrass festivals and holding deep philosophical discussions while soaking in Steve and Janene's wood-fired hot tub.

On days when we were not cutting trees, Art and I began to scrape the bark off our logs, sort them according to size and flatten one side of each with a chainsaw.

* * *

As I stood on the roof of our workshop recalling these events and watching my sweat-drenched husband work on the hot slippery metal, I thought about the birds I could see and what they must do to support their lifestyles. They lead difficult and dangerous lives, spending their time avoiding danger, reproducing and raising young, foraging for food and migrating. But, they are not weighed down by possessions, their own procrastination and guilt, or the search for meaning.

Possessed

My house had more rooms than I remembered. One room led to another. Each room contained possessions I had forgotten about: clothes, dishes, photographs, old letters, books, beds, tables, chairs and couches. Each room contained a walk-in closet with more possessions. Sometimes the closets had doors to other closets. I had to sort through these possessions, but I couldn't make any headway and my mother was watching me.

This dream seemed to be playing itself out in real life.

* * *

After we had completed our roofing job, we steeled ourselves to face the interior of our workshop. The ceiling was in tatters; paneling hung down in chunks; pink fiberglass insulation with black paper backing hung down in strips, like giant batwings. Bats slept in nooks and crannies. Mouse feces covered everything, including Art's rusting tools. The drawers contained nests. Raccoon tracks reached up the walls. A house wren had made a nest inside one of the light fixtures.

We began by sorting through our possessions in the loft, which stretches over half of the shop. Art did some preliminary testing of his tools and found most of them salvageable.

The loft contained canning supplies I hadn't touched for 10 years, a rotting rocking chair, nests made out of fabric scraps, two broken end tables, a cracked mirror, glass that we had saved for window repair, oak and cherry lumber (some of it useable), a desk, two bicycles, two porta-potties and a bookcase full of woodworking supplies.

After completing the cleanup, we had a shamefuly large heap of trash and a 36 x 12-foot loft that looked good enough to live in. It occurred to me that people in developing nations would relish a living space like this.

Our next job was to pull down the insulation from the high open ceiling. The task looked impossible at first, but we had put the insulation up there and so it surely must be possible to take it down. We managed, as we usually did, working as a team, with Art doing the most skilled and dangerous part and me doing the grunt work, wrapping my arms around the scratchy feces-laden fiberglass and stuffing it into black plastic bags.

Next, I scraped a mixture of old sawdust, oil, mildew, mouse feces and who knows what else off the cement floor while Art sorted all his nails, screws, bolts and small tools, including those he had inherited from my dad.

Finally, we called Tony Severson of S & S Sanitation in Preston to haul away our trash, which included our 1980 Yamaha motorcycle that had been working its way into the earth for 10 years and whose only remaining value was sentimental.

Tony came twice with two pickup trucks and a trailer. He, his brother-in-law and Art piled our junk into his vehicles. Tony's six-year-old son, Adam, and I helped, too, although mostly we looked for butterflies and birds. As I watched our shameful pile disappear, it occurred to me that you could learn a lot about a person by looking at his trash.

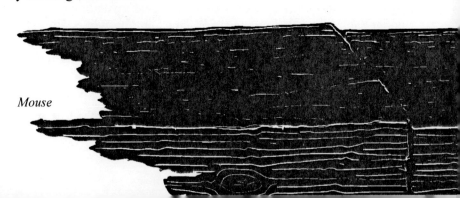

Mouse

When we finally got close to the bottom of our pile, we ran into a swarm of bees that stung all three men and required applications of wet baking soda to draw the stingers out.

The last task was to hook the trailer to one of the trucks, which little Adam did with surprising skill for a six-year-old.

In Fillmore County, no one finishes a job and just walks away, so when we had loaded the trucks and trailer, we took time to visit. We talked about the possibility that Waste Management, Inc. (WMI) would take over the Resource Recovery Center in Preston and Tony's fear that WMI would drive him out of business. We told him we were happy we didn't have to hire the expensive services of WMI for this job.

In spite of all our accomplishments in cleaning the workshop, my guilt-ridden dreams of rooms and possessions continued. I thought perhaps I would find peace once I sorted through the possessions in our house—the pots, pans, dishes, clothes, books . . .

Rose-breasted Grosbeak

Do you hear?
Or would you hear only
a sudden silence
drawing your eyes
to where he sits
his rose-colored heart
bleeding from his breast?
Would you miss
his black and white song
spilling across a blue sky?

*Rose-
breasted
Grosbeak in
Bur Oak*

Birds & The Ecology of Learning

In 1978, when we moved from Minneapolis to our house in the Big Woods, we placed two bird feeders on a poplar tree outside our kitchen window and one feeder on the ground near our pump. We knew almost nothing about birds, but had heard them singing in the woods.

We saw little flocks of bright yellow birds flying across the field near our house. We called them wild canaries. We also noticed rose-breasted grosbeaks, phoebes and indigo buntings, which we thought were bluebirds.

Black-capped chickadees and white-breasted nuthatches were the first to arrive at our feeders. Next came the cardinals, followed by downy and red-bellied woodpeckers, goldfinch (our wild canaries) and purple finch.

However, it was not until 1984 that we seriously turned our attention to birds. I began to take long walks in the woods, looking for birds. I learned the fundamentals of bird identification from a book, from other birders and by studying birds while out in the woods; binoculars in one hand, a guidebook in the other.

Bald Eagle

I did not learn from a book or through binoculars the things that can only be learned from the birds themselves. Among many things, the birds also taught me about the process of learning.

* * *

When I think it's time for the kinglets to pass through, I look and there they are. I know where a blue jay is before I see it. I know a bluebird will sing before I hear it. I'm not sure why this happens, but I have some ideas. The explanation includes the use of all of my senses, singly and in combination.

Raindrops on my tongue tell of spring and red-winged blackbirds; the sweet taste of blackcaps in July tell me about summer and robins; bitter cedar berries in fall recall cedar waxwings; and the crisp cold taste of January makes me wonder how birds survive a Minnesota winter.

The touch and smell of spring, the air on my skin, humid and soft, tells me to listen for the spring songs of chickadees, nuthatches, cardinals and the first migrating vireos and warblers, the gobbling of wild turkeys and the drumming of woodpeckers and ruffed grouse. My ears tune into sounds others don't hear, like the "wah-wah" call of a nuthatch. Sometimes a chickadee sings in January and, to me, it feels like spring.

The Chinese believe certain sounds can balance and heal. Bird songs balance and heal me.

* * *

My eyes note movements others don't see. One time, I caught something out of the corner of one eye. I was preoccupied with the tasks of the day as I walked the old tractor trail through the woods. I stopped to look at the bird I thought I saw; a great flapping of wings had given it away.

The bird was perched near the top of a broken tree about 30 feet from where I stood. Other trees stood between it and me, so it was hard to get a good look. "Red-tailed hawk," I thought, "they're common enough."

Then I saw a pair of feathered legs and enormous yellow talons kneading the tree like my cat kneads my lap. A bald eagle. As it turned toward me, I saw a white head, a dark brown breast, and whitish undersides of wings. I moved to get a better view, just as a second eagle joined the first.

The eagles stood there together on the tree flapping their wings. The first one lowered its head like a hissing cat and the second one flew away. I watched them fly low through the trees in opposite directions. Suddenly I saw them flying and tumbling high in the sky. Then I saw a third bird. Soon there were four of them calling, soaring and climbing, their majestic wings held perfectly straight. As they soared out of sight, I noticed my cheeks were wet and wondered why I was crying.

* * *

Birds can tell when to migrate by the light in the sky at certain times of the year. Do humans have a similar response, discarded as a mere feeling? One day in April, I felt an urgent need to get our bluebird house ready, to give it one last cleaning, pound the post deeper into the ground and put the door back on. When I was done and walking away, something told me to turn around. I looked and there was the bluebird pair, sitting on the house.

When I think it's time to see a hermit thrush, a look through binoculars proves me right. I hear calls and songs of birds I don't expect to recognize, but my hunches are usually correct. Is this intuition? Maybe so, but I don't believe there is anything super-natural about it. There are explanations, some that I know, some at which I can only guess. Perhaps I heard or saw the bluebirds earlier and tucked them away in my subconscious mind.

Perhaps it's the behavior of birds I recognize when I don't see well enough to identify markings. A hermit thrush flies from the underbrush to a branch low in a tree. It doesn't fly far at a time. When I loose track of it, I can usually find it again if I look care-fully nearby.

If I see a bird fly deep into brush where I can no longer see it, I think of a sparrow. If I see a very small bird fluttering its wings and flying quickly from perch to perch, I'm quite sure it's a kinglet. When I hear a high pitched chickadee-like sound, I know the kinglet is golden-crowned.

I don't know all the warbler songs, but I know when I'm hear-ing a warbler. I used to think any bird that sang a pretty song was a warbler. I didn't know that warblers are small colorful birds that migrate through this county on their journeys north in spring and south in fall. I didn't know that I would eventually identify, right here, 29 species of warblers and discover that five species breed here. Warblers fly quickly from place to place grabbing up insects, but they don't flutter their wings as kinglets do and they don't all have pretty songs.

When a bird flies out from the limb of a tree, grabs an insect, then flies back to the same perch, or a nearby one, I look for a phoebe, a pewee, or some other flycatcher. When I hear an indigo bunting sing, I look for him at the top of a small tree.

The rose-breasted grosbeak sings on his nest. Like clockwork, he appears at my kitchen window each spring on May 1.

I am no expert on birds, but I love what I've learned and I love knowing there is always more to learn. And it's interesting to know that I don't even consciously know all that I know. This gives me faith in myself and in my intuition.

At Home
in the Woods

Simply to be trusted by a shy wild creature enhances one's self-respect.

-Alexander Skutch

Alexander Skutch is one of the great naturalists of our time. Almost 70 years ago, he traveled to Central America to study plants, but the tropical birds there quickly captured most of his attention. For 10 years, he wandered around tropical America, living in research stations or rented cabins.

In 1941, he settled down on a farm he bought in a Costa Rican rain forest. Ahead of his time, he attempted to live and farm in a sustainable and ecologically sound manner, in harmony with the forest and its inhabitants. The great variety of plants and animals there has kept him busy for more than 60 years. At 96, he can still tell visitors which birds are nesting where, the number of eggs or nestlings in each nest, the behavior of the parents and the fate of the young.

Skutch is a prolific writer. His books and lifestyle have earned him high acclaim and have endeared him to birdwatchers around the world. In telling his own story, Skutch tells the stories of others as well, giving expression and understanding to the lives of his readers.

Skutch's essays in *A Naturalist on a Tropical Farm* (1980) seem to express the way that I feel about my life in the Big Woods which, in some ways, is similar to his life in Central America. As Skutch has traveled far on his farm, I have traveled far in the Big Woods of Fillmore County. I too spent much of my earlier life roaming about and, when it was time to settle down, I looked diligently for the place that might fulfill my dreams.

Since moving to the Big Woods, I have found little need to leave. The woods offers me so much that I hardly need more. At the right time of the year, I can step outside and see yellow-bellied sapsuckers tapping on their favorite elm and ruby-throated hummingbirds frequenting the same trees for sap pooling in the woodpecker holes. I can walk down my driveway and see waves of migrating warblers, thrushes and sparrows. I can sit on the banks of the South Fork and watch flocks of robins, cedar waxwings, golden-crowned kinglets, ruby-crowned kinglets and yellow-rumped warblers.

Like Skutch, I have an emotional attachment to my woods and have learned much of what I know about it through careful observation. I feel proud when a chickadee lands on my hand or a deer comes within touching distance. Sometimes I look so long at the bur oak beside my porch that I seem to enter its burly bark. Like Skutch, I know the importance of details; I've spent hours observing and describing the colors, veins and passage of time in a single leaf.

I have a particular affinity to northern cardinals, who, like me, form long-term pair bonds with their mates and rarely leave their own territories. Cardinals are easy to observe because they come to our feeders every day of the year. Females have pink beaks and plumage showing subtle shades of red, green, gray and buff. Male beaks are red; male plumage is bright red.

Cardinals counter-sing with their mates. One bird sings a certain phrase several times and the other matches it. When the leader changes to a new phrase, the other matches it again. At breeding time, the birds engage in mate feeding; the male picks up a bit of food, hops over to the female and the two touch beaks as she takes the food.

Cardinals have as many as four broods in a season. Juveniles have dark beaks and plumage similar to their mothers. Male cardinals are attentive, almost compulsive, caregivers. In addition to feeding their own young, they often feed the young of other species. Unfortunately, it is not unusual to see them raising and feeding the young of the parasitic brown-headed cowbird.

Sometimes I watch and listen to the cardinals so intently that I feel as though I understand them, that I am almost one of them. Skutch's writing makes me believe he has also had this kind of experience.

Northern Cardinal

In *The Minds of Birds* (1996), he writes:

"It is remarkable how often the sounds that birds make suggest the emotions that we might feel in similar circumstances; soft notes like lullabies while calmly warming their eggs or nestlings; mournful cries while helplessly watching an intruder at their nests; harsh or grating sounds while threatening or attacking an enemy; sharp, castanetlike clacking of the bill while trying to intimidate a rival or interloper. Birds so frequently respond to events in tones such as we might use that we suspect their emotions are similar to our own."

I am grateful to Alexander Skutch for giving me words to express my own experience and perhaps, in turn, the opportunity to ignite a similar passion in someone else.

Anne Marie

One day in the summer of 1987, my husband and I went hiking in Beaver Creek State Park in Houston County. When I stopped to look for the blue-gray gnatcatchers I heard whispering in the treetops, I saw a man and a woman with binoculars around their necks walking toward me. They stopped to talk and I learned for the first time about the Minnesota Ornithologists' Union (MOU), a statewide birding organization.

As soon as I arrived back home, I sent for membership information. I had been birding on my own for four years; it was time to join a group.

Not long after the Beaver Creek encounter, I received a call from Anne Marie Plunkett, who would become my first birding mentor. Anne Marie is a skillful, passionate birder from Rochester. Because she had been researching the life and journals of Johan C. Hvoslef, Lanesboro physician and naturalist from 1876 to 1920, she had a particular interest in Fillmore County.

Her first comment when she visited our woods was, "I think I died and went to heaven." From Anne Marie, I quickly learned how much I didn't know about birds. She was a gentle and careful teacher.

On January 2, 1988, Fillmore County had its first Christmas Bird Count (CBC). Anne Marie arranged everything: the publicity, routes, meeting place and lunch.

CBCs take place every year all across the Americas. More than 45,000 people participate in day-long counts of winter birds. The results become part of the longest running database in ornithology, representing nearly 100 years of unbroken data. The first CBC took place on Christmas Day 1900, when ornithologist Frank Chapman, an officer in the budding Audubon Society, suggested counting birds as an alternative to the annual Christmas bird shoot.

Each count lasts one day and must occur sometime between mid-December and mid-January. Participants count numbers and species of birds within a 15-mile radius of a central location. Our base for the first count was the Root River Trail Headquarters in Lanesboro. A total of 30 participants—including people from Fillmore County, Rochester, Stewartville and Minneapolis—counted 45 species. Some of the highlights were two rough-legged hawks, wild turkeys, gray partridge, an eastern screech owl, a pileated woodpecker in downtown Lanesboro, a golden-crowned kinglet and snow buntings.

Anne Marie called me a few days after the count. Little did I know that she was about to push me out of the nest. When she

Golden-crowned Kinglet

asked me to organize a meeting to form a bird club, I couldn't say no, but I was worried. She apparently had not noticed my social anxiety—or maybe she had and thought this task would be good for me.

Our first meeting was February 20, 1988 in Lanesboro. Nearly 20 people attended, including some who have since become good friends and birding partners. At the meeting, I offered to coordinate activities and edit a newsletter. Anne Marie volunteered to be our MOU representative. I met my second mentor, Dr. Alden Risser, at this session.

During the next two years, we had two more CBCs and field trips that took us all over the county: Kappers' and Department of Natural Resources (DNR) ponds near Spring Valley, Sumner Township, Cabbage Rocks near Highland, our Big Woods, the Root River Trail, the Eagle Bluff Environmental Learning Center north of Lanesboro and Forestville State Park.

Although she organized our second CBC, Anne Marie was weaning the Fillmore County Birders from her watchful care. Nevertheless, our friendship continued. She is the person I call when I have an identification question. She was the first person I notified the spring I saw a hooded warbler on my land and the winter I saw pine grosbeaks in our red cedars.

Anne Marie is generous with her time and resources. In 1989, she gave me a MOU field trip. I chose a May trip to Winona and Houston Counties, about 45 miles east of us, bordering the Mississippi River. I was anxious because I wouldn't know anyone on the trip, but I was lucky. The first person I met was Alice Hennessey from Minneapolis, who invited me to ride with her and her friends. Although we live three hours apart, Alice and I still keep in touch and bird together a couple times a year.

I also met Carol Schumacher on this field trip. She would become my third mentor, seven years later. In the summer of 1996, just after I joined the Winona Audubon Club, Carol arrived at my house to re-introduce herself and see the woods that Anne Marie had told her were like heaven. By then, Anne Marie had become Carol's mentor, too. The world is smaller than I thought.

Doc Risser

On May 14, 1988, Stewartville doctor, Alden Risser, led the Fillmore County Birders through his favorite birdwatching place, the Cabbage Rocks area in the Big Woods near Highland. Dr. Risser had warned us this would be a rigorous hike through woods, over rocks and across streams. Only eight of our original 20 hikers lasted the entire trip. By the end of the day, we had seen 74 species of birds.

As we searched for birds, the youngest members of our group, John and Chris Hockema, imitated the buzzy song of a blue-winged warbler, a lively little bird with a bright yellow crown, throat and breast, a black eyeline and blue-gray wings. It is one of 35 warbler species that migrate into or through southeastern Minnesota each spring and fall.

Chris located an answering bird, but said it looked different; it had a black throat and black patches on both cheeks. Doc knew immediately it was a Lawrence's warbler, the rare hybrid of a blue-winged and golden-winged warbler, and one of the rarest birds he'd ever seen. He told us that it was his birthday and the sighting was a perfect gift.

* * *

In 1929, Dr. Risser was one of nine founding members of the Upper Mississippi Bird Club. The name of the club was soon changed to the Minnesota Bird Club. In 1931, Doc became secretary-treasurer of the club. From 1932-1933, he was editor of its magazine, *The Flicker*, and in 1935, he became club president. In 1938, the Minnesota Bird Club joined with the T. S. Roberts Ornithology Club of St. Cloud and the Duluth Bird Club to form the Minnesota Ornithologists' Union.

During these years, Doc kept a journal in which he noted his companions, as well as details of his observations of flora and bird species. In the preparation of his classic work, *The Birds of Minnesota* (1932), Dr. Thomas Roberts made extensive use of Doc's observations.

When I met Doc, he was in his mid 70s and still a practicing physician. He had been mentoring other birdwatchers since he was a young man. Although all the Fillmore County Birders were his protégés, he was more than a birding mentor to John and Chris; he was like a father. They first met at the Sumner Center

*Blue-winged Warbler
in Black Oak*

United Methodist Church where the boys' grandmother introduced them. Their first field trip together was to Forestville State Park in 1984.

* * *

On April 29, 1989, Gordy and Mary Jo Dathe of Spring Valley led a field trip around western Fillmore County. As we crossed a field to the edge of a woodlot, Doc forged ahead, bent forward, binoculars held ready. When the rest of us caught up, we found him watching an early brown thrasher. We watched the thrasher with Doc, then walked into the woodlot.

Someone looked up and spotted an occupied hawk's nest. Doc identified the bird as a Swainson's hawk, unusual for the area. The Dathes and Hockema brothers kept watch on the bird, her mate, and progeny for years to come. Ten years later, a Swainson's hawk was still nesting there.

On May 13, 1989, we were with Doc again at Cabbage Rocks. It had been one year since we had seen the Lawrence's warbler.

Bloodroot

We wondered if we would see it again. If we did see it, would it be the same bird as the year before?

We heard a buzzy sound. There it was—black cheeks, black throat, bright yellow head and breast and blue wings. We watched transfixed for a moment, losing ourselves and melting into our surroundings. We became Shattuck Creek, working her way to the Mississippi. We were a wood thrush song, a finger of sun opening a bloodroot flower, a spider's web swinging in a light breeze. The moment passed and we came back to ourselves, but some of the magic remained as we continued on our way.

* * *

As I became better acquainted with Doc, I learned that he never watched birds in a vacuum; he was always part of his surroundings, never merely an observer. He was a religious man, for whom birding was a spiritual experience.

Once, when he was hiking alone in an English woods, he came upon a clearing and sat down on a stump to eat his lunch. Several small English birds, much like our chickadees, approached him. He held out bits of food in his open hand, tempting the birds to come closer. Soon he felt the feathery touch of tiny feet on his hand, his head and hopping up and down his outstretched arm. I can imagine Doc sitting there like that—St. Francis of Assisi reincarnated in an English forest.

In 1995, in his early 80s, Doc retired from his practice and moved with his wife to Minneapolis. He was no longer able to forge ahead, leaning forward, binoculars held ready, but he could still walk short distances. In the spring of 1999, John Hockema walked with him in the Robert's Bird Sanctuary in Minneapolis. He said Doc was in good spirits.

On December 5, 1999, Doc passed away. Among the hundreds of mourners at his memorial service were his family members, birdwatchers, patients, co-workers and members of his church.

I know I can never see Doc again, but I still half expect to wake up on a Saturday morning, look out my kitchen window and see the boys and him standing in my driveway, binoculars to their eyes.

The Great Bird Day

In 1872, at the age of 33, Dr. Johan Christian Hvoslef came to this country from his native Norway. He had received an education in general sciences at the University of Norway in Oslo and, when he arrived in America, he attended Rush Medical College in Chicago. In 1876, he came to Lanesboro, where he practiced medicine until his death on October 11, 1920. By most accounts, he was a dour person with little sense of humor and may have felt superior to his patients and the people of Lanesboro.

He married Karen Anderson of Lanesboro and they had one child, a daughter named Agnes. The doctor doted on his little girl and was heartbroken when she died of pneumonia at the age of six and a half. From the time of her death in 1898 until his own death in 1920, he visited Agnes' grave every day, bringing fresh flowers and tending to the site. The Hvoslef family marker and two small markers, one for Agnes and one for the doctor, still stand in the Lanesboro Cemetery. There is no marker at the site for the doctor's wife.

In addition to practicing medicine, Dr. Hvoslef was a wild bird enthusiast who completed more than 50 journals of his daily activities, the weather and his observations of nature, particularly birds, in Fillmore County. He gathered and prepared more than 400 bird skins, some of which now belong to the Bell Museum at the University of Minnesota. As was the custom in the late 1800s, he acquired the skins by shooting the birds.

Following Agnes' death, he continued with his observations, but gave up his gun. He also began writing in English, instead of Norwegian.

From the journals of Dr. Johan Christian Hvoslef, Diary #10:

"Thursday, October 5, 1911 The great bird day: This morning 38 degrees and it looked as if the long period of rain at last had come to an end. I went to 'the hill' and took fresh flowers along. It was so chilly that I hardly was able to handle the filled glass. By the gate, there were so many birds . . . In the valley and at the outlet, there it was swarming with birds. When I got home I was called to Miss Ole Carlsen near Pekin and drove there with livery team from M. Horihan, with Erik Bohn driving . . . At length the rain poured down and the roads became horrid. On the Casey hill met with an automob. in the deep clay mud. That ride could hardly have been very pleasant. ***The whole world, almost everywhere was swarming with birds.*** The following I was able to identify, but very many more species, of course, escaped my spying eyes.

[As was the custom in those days, Dr. Hvoslef used, almost exclusively, the scientific Latin names of the birds he saw.]

Robins, great flocks

Poocates, very many by the new school house [*Pooecetes* – vesper sparrow]

Dend coronata, in great numbers [Dendroica coronata – yellow-rumped warbler]

Spiz socialis, numerous [*Spizella socialis* – chipping sparrow]

Spiz pusilla, and there were undoubtedly others. [*Spizella pusilla* – field sparrow]

Colaptes [flicker]

Bonasa at two places in the valley [*Bonasa umbellus* – ruffed grouse]

Junco, very many, everywhere

Siala, very many [*Sialia sialis* – eastern bluebird]

Accipit coopery (male) dived down among bushes full of small birds, and at once everything became as still as the grave. [*Accipiter cooperii* – Cooper's hawk]

Spinus tristis, many [*Spinus tristis* – American goldfinch]

Zonotr. albicol., countless myriads [*Zonotrichia albicollis* – white-throated sparrow]

There und. [undoubtedly. *ed.*] were the *Zon. leu.* I was unable to determine this in our hurried passing by. [*Zonotrichia leucophrys* – white-crowned sparrow]

Pipilo several LAST [*Pipilo* – towhee]. [LAST refers to his last sighting for 1911]

Very many crows.

I also believe I saw some *Otocoris*, but this is doubtful. [*Otocoris* – horned larks]

Melosp fasciata [*Melospiza fasciata* – song sparrow]

Melosp georgiana. undoubtedly. [*Melospiza georgiana* – swamp sparrow]

Passerella, a few [*Passerella iliaca* – fox sparrow]

Certhia, one, the river was getting higher. [*Certhia familiaris* – brown creeper]

Troch. not by the house. [*Trochilidae* – hummingbird species]

From Dagboks [Diaries] 1 and 2:

"Friday, June 30, 1882: "Last night we had the most awful storm that I've ever lived through in the United States. When I this morning, after a sleepless night, went out at six o'clock I found the river higher than I've ever seen it before. To reach here from Brooklyn [an area of Lanesboro] one has to use a boat. In the powder house the water reached almost halfway up the windows. With violent force the waters of the flood rush over the highway and under the trestle, the latter almost hidden under the water. The grand iron bridge by Iverson's is wrecked, and the same is true of the bridge leading to North Prairie. The trestle-work beyond the railroad bridge is ruined. All mail and telegraph communication with the rest of the world is cut off. The Thompson dam is out, and the roads are impassable for all vehicles. The heat is oppressive. Everyone dreads the coming of darkness. The riff-raff keeps up an uninterrupted racket with their

firecrackers in our poor town, and there is other devilishness going on . . .

"Monday, Oct. 30, 1882: Called to Rushford. A lot of the *Colinus* [bobwhite] are being shot on the plain above the town. On the river, there are many ducks. GR. shot eight of them. And there are beavers. Gr. caught one of them.

"Saturday, November 4, 1882: Last night I was called to Highland Prairie. To Paul P. Braaten's. Lovely, starry, moonlit night. Cold and frosty. Around three o'clock the glorious comet was visible though it now seems considerably smaller and dimmer over the horizon. It is said that many prairie chickens are dying on Highland Prairie. An elk—just like something miraculous—is down in the woods. Quail and partridge in considerable numbers.

"Thursday, April 12, 1883: Overclouded, gray, and cold. The prairie chickens boomed so loudly this morning from Henrik's field that we could hear them very plainly in town. Never before have I heard anything like this."

[Prairie chickens disappeared from Fillmore County in the late 1930s. These birds were hunted in Minnesota until 1942. The highest number, 410,000, was taken in 1925.]

Great Prairie Chicken

In his classic work, *The Birds of Minnesota* (1932), Dr. Thomas S. Roberts drew heavily on Dr. Hvoslef's journal records. In his introduction, he wrote that all the Lanesboro records in his book were taken from Dr. Hvoslef's notes and that Dr. Hvoslef had probably done more than any other person to contribute information to the bird-life in a single locality.

* * *

Anne Marie Plunkett attempted to fill the data void created by the death of Dr. Hvoslef. Over a period of several years in the 1980s, she saw and identified 240 species of birds in Fillmore County, more than any other individual has ever recorded here. In addition to studying the birds, she gathered local anecdotes and reviewed the Hvoslef journals, located in the archives of the University of Minnesota in Minneapolis. One persistent local anecdote she encountered is that the doctor talked to his deceased daughter through a drainage pipe near her grave.

On October 5, 1986, exactly 75 years after the doctor's "great bird day," Anne Marie attempted to recreate that day by retracing the doctor's footsteps and recording all the birds she saw. She began with a trip to the Lanesboro Cemetery, where she placed flowers on little Agnes' grave. Rain fell off and on, as it had in 1911.

Anne Marie followed the former main road from Lanesboro to Preston, a road Dr. Hvoslef frequently walked, and then drove from Lanesboro to Pilot Mound (previously Pekin) where she encountered the "deep clay mud" referred to in the journal. She saw most of the same birds Dr. Hvoslef had seen, plus flocks of European starlings, which were not in Lanesboro during the doctor's time.

* * *

In October 1996, Dr. Kinsey Anderson (formerly of Preston, Minnesota, now of El Cerrito, California) and his wife Lilica donated 204 acres of land in the Big Woods of Fillmore County to the state of Minnesota. Dr. Anderson asked to have the resulting Wildlife Management Area (WMA) named in honor of Dr. Hvoslef as a preserve for wildlife, particularly songbirds. He asked the Department of Natural Resources (DNR) to work with the Minnesota Ornithologists' Union (MOU) to develop management plans. He also requested hunting restrictions to accommodate spring and fall birding activities.

Dr. Anderson is the son of Moppy Anderson, former state legislator and Preston resident who, over time, bought the numerous plots that now comprise this WMA. At its dedication on May 3, 1997, Dr. Anderson spoke fondly of his boyhood days spent exploring the property and observing its wildlife.

Following the dedication, area residents, MOU members and DNR officials formed a committee to discuss management plans. At the first meeting, Carrol Henderson, State DNR Nongame Wildlife Manager and Bob Janssen, former MOU president, advised on the need for systematic yearly bird counts, including a breeding bird survey and a checklist of species found during each season.

Carrol Henderson also reviewed Dr. Hvoslef's work and journals at the meeting. Out of this meeting, interest grew in obtaining copies of the original journals from the University of Minnesota, approximately half of which are in Norwegian, with the intention of transcribing and translating them.

Committee members decided they would like to initially publish the journals verbatim and later produce a book that would contain biographical and historical information, journal excerpts, old maps, photographs and illustrations. Nancy Bratrud, a friend and a Big Woods neighbor of mine, offered to pursue the matter.

* * *

On one of our birding trips together, I showed Dana Gardner around the Hvoslef WMA. We went to the old farm pond where I once watched a solitary sandpiper ride a floating log, the field where bobolinks sing and the tops of bluffs over which red-tailed hawks and bald eagles soar. We roamed the twisting and turning South Fork where trout swim and great blue herons fish, and Simley Springs where we stood immersed in the roar of water tumbling over rocks.

I told Dana about the Hvoslef journals, with which he was already familiar, and the plan to publish them. I asked if he would be interested in illustrating the journals and he agreed.

Dana's interest in the journals increased my own interest and gave me the ammunition to prod the DNR into action. On June 14, 2000, Jack Heather, a Minnesota DNR Wildlife Specialist, organized our third meeting, primarily to discuss the Hvoslef journals. Dana's illustrations, we all agreed, would add greatly to the value of the book, especially considering his ties to Lanesboro, the town where, as a child, he first became interested in birds.

Carrol Henderson said he could make some DNR funds available for the project. I mentioned Anne Marie Plunkett's previous interest in Dr. Hvoslef and suggested her as a possible resource. Those who already knew of Anne Marie agreed that we should invite her to become part of the project.

A few days later, I called Anne Marie. Although we had been out of touch for several years, we were able to pick up where we had left off. In response to my questions about Dr. Hvoslef, she related some interesting anecdotes and agreed to act as a consultant to the project. She said she had wanted to pursue further study of the journals and Dr. Hvoslef's life but in the 1980s, she could find no other interested parties and the project was too large for one person.

When Dana returned for a visit to Lanesboro in October, I arranged for Nancy Bratrud, Dana and I to meet Anne Marie for lunch and an afternoon of retracing some of the doctor's footsteps. Our first stop was the Lanesboro Cemetery and the Hvoslef family plot. We then drove the old main road from Lanesboro to Preston, where we saw some of the same birds the doctor and Anne Marie had seen.

We talked about Dr. Hvoslef's uncanny ability to reach beyond the grave to bring together historians, naturalists, an artist, writers and philanthropists. To bring his legacy full circle, it seemed only fitting that we should do what we could to make his journals available to the public.

Hvoslef Journals

Whenever I stand at the Hvoslef plot in the Lanesboro Cemetery, high above the town, I feel as though I have visited the place more times than I actually have. The plot stands on a hillock, a little aside from the other plots along the cemetery road. The fir trees from Dr. Hvoslef's time are still there, but the black walnuts that the doctor planted are gone.

I try to imagine the scene as it once was, with just one marker, that of little Agnes, dated January 31, 1892 - June 2, 1898. I try to imagine the plot with fresh bouquets and flowers planted by a grieving father—the carnations, dahlias, chrysanthemums, dianthus, verbenas, geraniums, as well as a mountain ash tree. I try to imagine the bushes in which the doctor found so many small birds.

But there are no flowers, only a carpet of mowed grass. And there is another marker here, that of Dr. Johan C. Hvoslef, September 7, 1840 - October 20, 1920.

* * *

For several years, I worked with Dr. Hvoslef's journals. I had eagerly accepted when the Journals Committee offered me the job of transcribing all of the diaries written in English.

Following negotiations with University of Minnesota archivist Penelope Krosch, Nancy Bratrud and I had received permission to bring all 57 notebooks on loan to Lanesboro, where they would be easily accessible to us.

As preliminary work on the project, I catalogued each notebook according to dates and with information on size and various idiosyncrasies. I researched the birds, plants and other wildlife that Dr. Hvoslef reported and matched the Latin names he used with present day Latin names and common names.

After completing the preliminary work, I began to transcribe page by page. The work was difficult; the doctor wrote in pencil and his handwriting was hard to decipher.

I was immediately struck with the depth of the doctor's grief over the loss of his daughter. Following her death, he began a ritual of daily walks from his house in the north part of Lanesboro to the cemetery at the southern end of town, which he euphemistically called "the hill." There, he visited his daughter's grave, which he always referred to as "the place." As part of the ritual, he entered daily accounts of his visits in his diary.

From Diary #3:

> *Saturday, July 30, 1904:* A very warm close night and morning. But it did not rain during the night. Very dark and for the first time I had to use the lantern also to light my lamps at the office. Got up at 4 o'clock. It is now after 5 o'clock and yet I cannot see writing without artificial light. Has just commenced thundering. Lightening and frequent peals of thunder are resounding through the dark, close air. It is undoubtedly a severe storm that is coming—is raining and thundering. Very dark and close. The rain had stopped when I went to "the hill": changed water, watered, weeded, etc, cut grass . . . A *Trochilus* [hummingbird] flew by. Getting very watery. A hot south wind is blowing. A very warm, sultry afternoon. In the morning and forenoon much noise of *Progne* [purple martins].

As I worked, I readily identified with the doctor's intensity, shyness, sadness, passion for birds and methodical recording of details. He seemed to be the happiest when observing nature out in the countryside or studying the specimens he brought home. Nothing escaped his curious eyes. He studied flowers, grasses, trees, fish, snakes, insects, mammals, birds and the sky. He often described the birds and the weather in a poetic manner. He freely expressed his opinions on local and world events. His recording of daily activities and observations gives an idea of life in Fillmore County in the late 1800s and early 1900s.

I loved the sense of continuity I felt as Dr. Hvoslef's words flowed through my fingers into the modern day world.

From Diary # 3:

> *Sunday, Aug. 21, 1904:* Was up a little after 4 o'clock. A very warm night and morning. Heavy clouds and it looks like a storm. It commenced thundering and raining. And soon stopped again and I got off for "the hill." Looked very threatening, but I escaped . . . Saw many *Chaetura* [chimney swifts]. CYCLONE Minneapolis— St. Paul!

> *Sunday, Sept. 4, 1904:* On account of the Sammy show several watchmen guarded the town last night, and I found them when I got up at 4 o'clock. Weed took me around in the Sammy show . . . Already now at 5 o'clock the streets are alive with talk and laughter, the cocks are crowing and the ducks squawking—all of it probably in honor of Sammy the big politician.

[The Sammy show was a political rally for a local politician.]

> *Thursday, Jan. 12, 1905:* Very many farmers in town despite the great masses of snow and the mountainlike drifts. They are hardy people!

> *Thursday, Feb. 9, 1905:* **15 degrees F.** at 5 o'clock. The snow now is so enormously deep that I hardly shall be able to get to "the hill" today. Yet it is still, calm. Went to wife of Anders Darin and from there I got to "the hill." Such masses of snow probably never before seen in America.

Going Underground

One Saturday afternoon, I gathered a big pile of clothes, put them in my washing machine, added soap and turned on the water. I ignored the fact that the machine sounded different than usual; I went outside to scrub the birdbath. I ignored the fact that the pump sounded different—until the water stopped running altogether. I checked the electric box and saw that the circuit breaker was off. I switched the breaker back on and it kicked out. I tried again; the same thing happened.

When my husband arrived home, he could tell by the look on my face that something was wrong. He knew he had two jobs at hand—one to deal with my anxiety and the other to fix what caused it.

He first checked for obvious problems, but found nothing. He said he would have to wait until morning to check things out thoroughly. I pulled my soap-soaked clothes out of the washing machine and hung them up to dry.

My four pop bottles of standby water probably wouldn't see us through the night. We looked around for good water containers, but didn't find any. Our neighbors, the Ericksons, loaned us their containers and gave us water. It was back to the old days, some 20 years earlier, before we had a well—except this time we hauled water from the neighbors, instead of from our spring along the Big Woods road. Another difference was that we were a quarter century older and water felt much heavier than it used to.

Without the convenience of running water, it took me two hours to wash dishes. Nearing the end of the task, I became more efficient as I begin to recall the way I had washed dishes in the past.

Of course, we didn't have the use of our toilet, either. It had been a long time since we'd had to pee in a jar.

On Sunday morning, Art determined that the trouble was not above ground. Our 24-year-old pump had probably pumped for the last time. It was a relief to know the worst.

We called Larson Well Drilling of Mabel, the company that had drilled our well 24 years before. They remembered us and said someone would be out Monday morning at eight o'clock with a new pump. I poured out remaining water into old ice cream pails, pop bottles and jars. I returned to Erickson's with the empty jugs, saying to myself, "I will never be without water again."

I kept expecting other things to go wrong and was continually surprised that our car, electricity, gas heat, computers and telephone were still working.

On Monday morning at eight o'clock, two young men arrived in a large truck with a hoist. They pulled heavy-duty wiring and eleven 21-foot pipes out of the wellhead. I saw that the term "pulling a pump" has a literal meaning.

The old pump was attached to the last pipe, which was 238 feet below ground, poking through the limestone bedrock and into the Jordan sandstone formation. The well was cased and grouted to this point. Beyond, there was an open hole going into the Franconia formation 280 feet below ground, nearly as deep as the length of a football field.

According to the 1995 *Geologic Atlas: Fillmore County, Minnesota*, analyses show that the water in these aquifers could be as much as 35,000 years old. This means that their recharge from above-ground sources occurred so long ago that they are not likely to be contaminated. However, they could become contaminated over a long period of time, as polluted water closer to the surface will eventually recharge them.

The workers attached the new pump and the wiring to the last pipe and began the reverse procedure of lowering the pump 238 feet. By 10:30 a.m., the job was done. Our first water came out gritty and brown; it began to run clear a couple hours later.

I thought it was interesting that our access to this ancient water wouldn't exist without modern technology, without modern drills, hoists or electricity. Art smiled as I began to talk philosophically about our physical and spiritual connection to the underworld.

Karst Country

Regional Ground Water Specialist Jeff Green stood in a hole, looking up at the participants in a field trip sponsored by Fillmore County Water Planning. We were in the Cherry Grove Blind Valley Scientific and Natural Area (SNA), a 40-acre parcel in western Fillmore County recently acquired by the Minnesota Department of Natural Resources (DNR).

Jeff described the forces that had led to the formation of the area and its high concentration of sinkholes. The depression he was standing in was a blind valley and the entrance to a cave.

We looked across the depression, to layers of rock and a thin layer of soil that rose about 10 feet above us. Jeff invited us to climb down into the cave, where we soon arrived at a metal gate that barred us from further exploration. The gate was there to protect visitors from the deep water that runs through the cave after a heavy rain or sudden thaw.

Jeff explained that these 40 acres were ideal for the study of ground water and karst geology. The preservation of this site as an SNA would help maintain water quality in this and adjoining areas.

I had been a member of the Fillmore County Water Planning Citizens' Advisory Committee for almost a year. I understood that the county's karst topography made the interconnections between surface water and ground water complex and unpredictable, making our water resources vulnerable to contamination. Despite this background, I had only a minimal understanding of karst and had not understood Jeff's explanations.

After the field trip, I made a determined effort to learn more about Fillmore County's geology and its implications for water resources. My references for this study were: *The Geologic Atlas: Fillmore County, Minnesota, 1995*; *Billions of Years in Minnesota: The Geological Story of the State* by Edmund C. Bray (1985); *Minnesota at a Glance: Quaternary Glacial Geology* by B.A. Lusardi (1997); *Minnesota at a Glance: Ancient Tropical Seas—Paleozoic History of Southeastern Minnesota* by A.C. Runkel (2000).

During my explorations, I visited the offices of the Minnesota Geological Survey in St. Paul. There, I talked with John Mossler, manager of the Fillmore County project, and Howard Hobbs, research geologist and author of the surficial geology section of the atlas. The two brought me up to date on the latest thinking on the county's geology.

Later, during the grand opening of a traveling karst exhibit developed by the Science Museum of Minnesota and sponsored by the Southeast Minnesota Water Resources Board, I was able to visit with keynote speaker Dr. Calvin Alexander of the University of Minnesota Department of Geology and Geophysics. Dr. Alexander is the author of the section, "Karst— Aquifers, Caves and Sinkholes" in the *Geologic Atlas: Fillmore County.* He graciously answered my questions on the topographic features of karst and the influence of the ice ages.

* * *

One out of every four persons worldwide lives in a karst terrain; this terrain is present in all nine counties of southeastern Minnesota, in 20 percent of the land surface in the United States and 10 percent of the surface of the earth.

Karst terrain has distinctive drainage characteristics, due to a greater degree of rock solubility in natural waters than that found elsewhere. The soluble rocks must lie close to the surface, covered by less than 50 feet of glacial till or topsoil.

Fillmore County contains more karst features than the rest of Minnesota combined. Not all karst terrain looks like Fillmore County, however; the entire state of Florida has a karst terrain with abundant springs bubbling up from a flat landscape.

Karst areas have subsurface drainage that leaves minimal standing or flowing surface water. Much of Fillmore County has little natural surface water; smaller surface watercourses have flowing water for only a few hours after a major rainstorm or sudden thaw.

Underground, karst terrain can include: stream sinks (disappearing streams and stream sieves), blind valleys (stream valleys with no surface water outflow), springs and seep points.

In karst terrain, any rainfall not lost to evaporation quickly sinks underground via infiltration through the thin layer of soil and runoff into sinkholes, stream sinks, and joints on exposed bedrock surfaces. Once in the subsurface, karst ground waters can flow rapidly through complex conduit systems that behave much like underground piping systems, featuring underground rivers and caves.

Sinkholes are closed depressions that function as connections between surface and ground waters, allowing surface water to flow into the subsurface. Fillmore County probably contains more than 10,000 active sinkholes, ranging from nuisances to hazards. Most are between 10 to 40 feet in diameter and are 5 to 40 feet deep.

Sinkholes form where water-borne sediment sinks or subsides through channels, such as joints and cracks in the underlying bedrock, resulting in erosion and voids in the subsurface. Collapses of cavities in the bedrock itself are rare.

If the erosion is slow compared to the rate of land surface adjustment, a slow subsidence sinkhole forms. If the erosion is rapid, the subsurface void can fail suddenly and a catastrophic sinkhole can appear. A catastrophic sinkhole may periodically collapse again, or may continue to grow by subsidence. Other sinkholes may begin with subsidence and later collapse catastrophically.

Both catastrophic collapse and slow subsidence can damage buildings on top of sinkholes. Water storage structures are especially prone to such damage. Facilities containing liquid wastes, such as manure lagoons and sewage ponds, require extraordinary precautions if constructed in high probability sink-hole areas, due to the high risk for contamination if the facility fails and its contents enter the environment.

Underground rivers are largely inaccessible, except where they flow through a cave. These rivers resemble surface rivers in map view. Small conduits gather water from sinkholes, stream sinks, stream sieves and water that infiltrates through the soil into the fractured bedrock. The small conduits combine downstream into larger conduits, and most return to the surface in springs.

Caves are cavities that have grown large enough for human entry and exploration; any dissolution of carbonate rock will form a cavity. Fillmore County has hundreds of caves, probably more than the rest of Minnesota combined. Some are dry for all or part of the year; others contain through-flowing streams. A cave may be a single passage with one connection to the surface, tubes with multiple branches, or large multi-level mazes with many possible surface connections.

The only two caves in Minnesota open to tours are located in Fillmore County. Mystery Cave, part of Forestville State Park, is the longest cave in the state and has more than 12 miles of mapped passages. Niagara Cave, near Harmony, extends vertically through three rock formations and includes an underground river and a large waterfall.

* * *

Ground-water contamination is a major concern in Fillmore County, as it is in many karst areas of the world. Because water in near-surface karst aquifers generally shows evidence of surface contaminants, the Minnesota Well Code does not permit the drilling of wells in such aquifers. In Fillmore County, however, many older wells continue to pump water from these aquifers.

Over a long period, the water from the near-surface aquifers will recharge the deeper aquifers, potentially transferring contaminants to them. The karst effects can extend well beyond the aquifers. Ground water flowing through a karst aquifer, which commonly contains surface contaminants, can also move into adjacent non-karst aquifers.

Among the common contaminants are: agricultural chemicals; chemicals or bacteria leached from wastes placed in sinkholes; nitrates, bacteria and other pollutants from community drainfields, municipal waste treatment facilities and improperly constructed domestic drainfields; salt from road de-icing; chemicals leaching from landfills; and leakage from petroleum storage tanks, pipeline ruptures and transportation accidents.

* * *

Fillmore County's karst topography is a mixed blessing. The county's geological make-up offers a variety of habitats and provides homes to rare plants, birds, amphibians and reptiles. The bluffs, deep valleys, springs and spring-fed streams draw sightseers, hikers, birdwatchers, campers and fishermen. The caves provide adventure and access into the mythical underworld. At the same time, the karst areas create a nightmare of potential pollution problems for the county's water resources.

The Point

The Root River runs through Southeast Minnesota to the Mississippi River. The South Fork of the Root River flows into the Root. Blagsvedt Run, a spring-fed stream, drains into the Fork.

The stream cuts a valley. The Big Woods road runs through the valley. The valley and the road twist and turn around limestone bluffs. One of the bluffs juts out to a point.

If you climb to the top of the bluff, you have a coyote's eye view of the road and the stream. A rusty barbed wire fence cuts into the trees next to the road. An animal trail twists and turns for 50 paces on the other side of the wire, until it comes to a place where a fallen willow is working its way into the ground. If you sit on the willow, you can put your feet in the stream and wait there for the chickadees.

If you follow the stream, you can step softly to the point where a wall of limestone rock rises over a pool of clear water. Swaying vegetation makes the water glow greener than moss. Moss illuminates one side of a tree. About 18 inches from the tree, a plastic milk jug works its way into the ground. A dented gas can rusts six feet from the jug. The water reflects a tangle of fallen branches with rotting leaves, a corn cob, brown fungus that looks like leather, white fungus that looks like shredded paper and a piece of scat that crumbles when you pick it up.

Sun shimmers on the water in shades of silver. Fish breath creates ripples from below. An insect dimples the pool with widening circles that create moving shadows on an overhanging branch. A spider's single strand joins one limb to another.

*Black-capped Chickadee
in White Oak*

Reflections

Mary came with me to the point below the bluffs along Blagsvedt Run. We sat on a branch, swinging our legs over the water. Brook trout hovered in the pool. A kinglet flashed his ruby crown. A chipmunk squealed. We heard a tractor purring on a hillside far across the valley and the metal wheels of an Amish buggy crunching gravel on the road.

"It all comes together here," I said. "It's synchronicity."

"Mere coincidence," said Mary, the scientist.

We looked down on our reflections in the pool. You could almost see the hairs on our legs. And the trees—all of their features showed—the leaves, the grooved bark and the woodpecker holes.

"If you look at it differently," I said, "you can see through the trees to the bottom of the pool, but you can't see both at once."

"This morning," said Mary, "I looked up from my desk and saw my neighbor cleaning her kitchen window. She didn't see me. She wasn't looking through the glass. She was looking at it."

We watched a red-tailed hawk circling over the bluffs.

"I dance up there," I said. "At the tip of the point, I forget myself and spread my wings. The red-tailed hawk laughs at me, but it's my dream and I can choose the roles I want to play."

Mary, the dancer, described leaving the floor. "I forget myself sailing through the air, looking back into the sky blue floor, hovering there lost in reflection."

"Are you more scientist or dancer?" I asked.

"I think the scientific method is a good way to approach almost anything. It teaches you the art of observation and you learn that the natural world is stranger and more complex than dreams or fantasy."

"I agree," I said, "but, there's more to a robin than a red breast—something the poet can state or the composer can express, something not scientific."

"You are right, of course," said Mary. "There are limits to science. Through science, we have learned that all things are connected. If a spider catches a butterfly, it affects the world economy. But, scientists cannot predict all the effects. Also, the scientific method does not produce music or poetry."

"I often contemplate cause and effect, order, and the connections between forces, geological features, plants and creatures," I said. "Sometimes, it seems to me that all things are only different manifestations of one phenomenon. Flocks of birds fly like waves of water, waves of sound or the grain in wood. You can look at the surface grain of wood, then you can look deeper and deeper, just as you can see through the trees to the bottom of the pool."

"Have you ever noticed how a twig looks like a small bone or how a Ping-Pong ball sounds like the drumming of a ruffed grouse?" Mary asked. "The trout below hover in the water like the red-tailed hawk up there hovers in air. The shadow in the pool mimics the trout and the trout's greenish body sways like moss. Have you ever seen a mink flowing like a shadow over the rocks?"

"If there is only one phenomenon," I said, "I suppose there is only one entity and we are all part of it. If so, how did the one thing divide into all the parts we see as separate? What is an entity, a flock of cedar waxwings, or only the individual birds?"

"Well, there are all kinds of entities," she said. "Birds and flocks, cells and organs, particles and waves, humans and societies. And they are all always changing, always evolving."

I knew we would get around to evolution at some point. It's one of our favorite topics.

Mary had recently given me the book *Darwin's Dangerous Idea* (1995), a meshing of science and philosophy, by Daniel C. Dennett. This book was particularly interesting to us—to Mary, the scientist, and me, the would-be philosopher.

Dennett, an analytical philosopher, wrote that scientists sometimes see philosophical ideas as having little to do with hard objective science and see themselves as immune from the confusions with which philosophers spend their whole lives. Dennett believes, however, that science is never free from philosophy and scientists who think it is have not examined their own philosophical baggage.

Dennett described the theory of evolution and then extended Darwin's vision to contemporary evolutionary biological theory. The book is technical, but accessible if one reads it very carefully. It took me a couple of months to get through half of it and it took

Eastern Chipmunk

Mary all of one summer to read it. She gave it to me as a vehicle to take our discussions to a new level.

"As you can imagine," I said, "I've been thinking a lot about evolution lately. I have a question for you. If several birds *choose* to sing more frequently than other members of their species and, if that choice promotes their well-being, will natural selection produce birds that sing more, thus making it part of their evolution?"

"I suppose so," she said. "That's almost Lamarckian, isn't it? Lamarck believed that acquired characteristics could be inherited. But, I think if we look carefully at your birdsong question, we'll find it fits Darwin's theory of natural selection, much of which has to do with chance and trial and error. You also have to investigate what caused the birds to sing more and there will be no easy answers to this question. Maybe the birds are singing more because they love to sing; maybe they need to sing more to establish territories in a densely populated area; or maybe the singing is part of a larger evolutionary trend."

"You're right, of course," I said. "Nothing is simple in totality, yet each small change is simple as can be. It's interesting to look at where life began and try to trace all the steps from that first species to the complexity of life as we know it now."

"I agree," she said. "The earliest forms of life were single-celled beings in the Pre-Cambrian time over 544 million years ago. Scientists were puzzled with the sudden appearance of multiple-celled entities in the Cambrian time. Now they're finding new links, multiple-celled beings and chordata with organs, that go back to the Pre-Cambrian."

"And we all came from that original spark of life and still share most of the same DNA," I said. "It's hard to believe that a virus came from the same place as me."

Dennett explained the process of speciation in terms of the algorithm, a formal logical process of very small steps that lead to a certain result. He said this was Darwin's dangerous idea—that evolution takes place by natural selection, a mindless, mechanical (algorithmic) process.

"Through Darwin's idea, Dennett makes you see the order inherent in the universe," I said. "Even chance has order. He comes close to explaining a beginning that doesn't include a kindly old man up in the sky."

"Yes," said Mary, "and that was a problem for Darwin. He didn't want to believe his own conclusions because they conflicted with his religious beliefs. And we know there are many today that still think his idea is heresy."

"What is really amazing is to think that a mindless mechanical process produced someone like Beethoven," I said. "I know that some of Beethoven's ability to compose came through learning and the evolution of culture and music, but his ability goes way beyond that."

Mary, the musician, said, "Beethoven is my favorite composer. I love to play his music; I experience it through my hands. Beyond that, words don't suffice. You like Wagner, don't you? He is too large for me. He takes forever to get to the point and I get bored."

"I do like Wagner," I agreed, "but Beethoven is my favorite composer now. I don't know why it took more than 50 years for me to be ready to hear him. He makes me feel like I've come home. At the same time, his genius makes him seem almost like another species. How can I have anything in common with him? I can more easily grasp my likeness to a virus."

"He composes like you write," she said. "Think about it. You're not so different. You go through the same process as Beethoven. The act of creation is similar in all humans and we're the only creatures who can indulge in this activity."

"Well, some people think that certain birds are creative," I said. "For example, the bower bird who creates elaborate nests, containing all kinds of trinkets, to entice a mate. But, I suppose this exception proves the rule."

"To create, you must be able to reflect, to see yourself in the universe," she said. "You must be conscious of yourself. As far as I know, humans, some primates and perhaps dolphins are the only creatures capable of self-consciousness."

"We are also the only creatures capable of drastically changing our environment," I said. "Sometimes I think self-consciousness is an evolutionary dead-end, that in the end, we will destroy not only ourselves, but the planet."

"You're not the only one who worries about that," she said. "I do too, but I still have faith in consciousness. I can't imagine a world without the creative impulse, without music, books, or paintings."

Suddenly, a monarch butterfly flew into a spider's web right in front of us. We stopped talking and watched. The spider zoomed down her silk super highway. She had an elliptical golden body; a yellow hump on her back; eight legs banded tan and black. She frantically wove the butterfly into her net.

Mary and I looked at each other, thinking we should not interfere. Let nature take her course. We waited, wondering who would be the first to give in.

I was the one. I watched my hand reach for the monarch and pluck it out of the web.

Blagsvedt Run

only brown trout can be seen from the sitting log
the brookies balance one foot over under cover
the willow supplies
a canopy of shade and web of roots
in the undercut bank

I altered the habitat
improvement for me
not the fish
so I could see better
I cut small branches and weeds

if the fish disappear it might be my fault
or light turning water into a mirror

Habitat Improvements

June, 1996

At one time, I viewed nature primarily in connection with birds. Then, one day, while sitting in the bluffs, mistaking the sound of the wind for the sound of birds, I found coyote scat and the wind suddenly sounded like howls. Hollow places in rocks turned into dens where I discovered bones. I looked for bones until I walked into a spider's web and began to see webs wherever I looked. A web of animal trails led me to a creek where I found brook trout in a web of roots, and then I began to see the connections in everything.

* * *

One day, I received a call from Kathy Bolin, Minnesota Department of Natural Resources (DNR) Non-game Resource Specialist. She said someone had told her that I had reported a Louisiana waterthrush on the stream running through my land. I said that I had seen a few.

She then described a controversy within the DNR regarding stream management. Historically, the Division of Fish and Wildlife had altered habitat in southeastern Minnesota streams to increase the carrying capacity of brown trout. Controversy had arisen over a stream management project in Beaver Creek State Park. The Division of Parks had objected to the harmful impact that the altered habitat could have on certain plant and bird species.

Kathy asked what I thought. Should they manage for trout, birds or plants?

"You have to consider all aspects," I said. "Everything is connected."

She asked if I wanted to go on a field trip to learn more about habitat improvement.

I agreed to the trip; I was very interested in the subject. I already knew something about habitat improvement. In 1994 and 1995, I had watched the DNR work on the South Fork of the Root River near my house. One day, as I was watching the birds, men and machines arrived with trucks full of rocks. The men smiled and waved. The birds flew away.

* * *

On field trip day, we met at the state fish hatchery in Lanesboro. DNR officials were there, as were fishermen, landowners and some of the state's top birders. We received diagrams of lunker units—which provide cover, sort of like an open cage—for trout. Each unit consists of oak blocks, oak stringers and reinforcing rods. A single unit is 4 x 5 feet. Once in place, it is covered with oak planks and riprapping (rock backfill).

Habitat improvement also includes the stabilization of eroded banks, the removal of woody debris and the elimination of new channel cuts and islands. This work results in increased stream flow and deeper water.

The success of a project is measured in number, size, and weight of the fish in the area. In one treatment zone, the number of trout before improvement was 94; the number after improvement was 507.

Our first stop was Diamond Creek, east of Lanesboro. In describing the history of the creek, our guide took us back to Indian times. He said we could never know for sure what it was like back then.

I thought, once man has put his mark on land, it can never go back to a natural state. When we talk about improvement, what does it mean? How can we know all the effects our actions will have? Should we leave the habitat alone, or can we correct previous mistakes?

We walked along the stream to observe the DNR work. Something moved on the far bank. We focused our binoculars, hoping to see a Louisiana waterthrush, a species in decline in North America. We saw a song sparrow instead.

Small numbers of the waterthrush—about 40 percent of all found statewide—nest in southeastern Minnesota, along eroded stream banks where exposed rocks and tree roots provide nesting sites. Six known pairs nested along Beaver Creek in 1995. The birds forage in streams on shallow cobbly substrates, fallen woody debris and emergent vegetation along the shores of banks and small islands.

There is a concern that habitat improvement for trout will destroy the habitat of the Louisiana waterthrush. It may also have adverse effects on the Acadian flycatcher (proposed state special concern), the cerulean warbler (federal candidate) and the rare native plants, such as the nodding wild onion.

* * *

The DNR formerly managed state lands for game animals, human recreation and commercially productive forests. Due to rising interest in non-game wildlife and increased knowledge of ecology, the focus has changed to ecosystem-based management.

The economic benefits of ecosystem management are not as immediately obvious as those of hunting and fishing. Sportsmen have always contributed to the conservation of game species. Trout stamps pay for habitat improvement; income from the sale of hunting and fishing licenses goes directly into the DNR.

But, others also contribute financially. Everyone who visits a state park pays for a park sticker. Participating manufacturers in the Wild Bird Food Program contribute two dollars to the DNR for each ton of feed sold, the Minnesota Ornithologists Union (MOU) supports a tax on birding supplies and Minnesota income tax forms offer an optional contribution to the Non-game Wildlife Fund (informally called the "Chickadee Check-off").

By the time of our field trip, ecosystem management had resulted in improved communication between parks and fisheries officials and with the public.

The improved communication had also helped with specific projects, such as finding a compromise solution for the Beaver Creek State Park stream management project. This compromise allowed the habitat where Louisiana waterthrush were known to nest to remain untouched, while habitat improvement for trout in other areas along the creek proceeded as planned.

It remained to be seen, however, if people like Jeff Broberg, President of the Minnesota Trout Association (MTA) would come around. In a Minnesota Trout Association newsletter, he had scorned ecosystem-based management and derided "tree-huggers" and "nature-fakers."

To him and everyone who thinks like him, I say that you have to see everything in relation to everything else. If we don't have balance, we don't have sustainability. And, if we don't have sustainability, we won't have anything in the end.

Louisiana Waterthrush

* * *

Forestville State Park, January 1998

Legislation added state forest land—including a large section of Canfield Creek—to Forestville State Park, in the western half of Fillmore County. At the request of the Minnesota Trout Association (MTA), District 32 State Senator Steven Morse wrote an exception into the legislation that gave control of the stream and 130 feet on either side of it to the Department of Fisheries.

In the belief that it would only have to deal with Fisheries, the MTA proposed a trout habitat improvement project for this area. However, the various DNR departments were working in concert at this time and all of them would be considering the proposal together, from all points of view.

Birding groups had historically opposed these types of projects, on the basis that they managed habitat exclusively for the non-native brown trout, while disrupting and altering the environment necessary for certain birds and native plant species.

On January 17, 1998, the DNR sponsored a meeting to discuss proposals for Forestville's South Branch Creek and Canfield Creek. The meeting began with MTA president Jeff Broberg recalling the controversy about Beaver Creek State Park and urging cooperation among all of the interested parties. He said the MTA's goals weren't so different from those of the other park users, since most fishermen also enjoy birds, plants and just being out in nature.

Another MTA representative, retired DNR Fisheries manager Mel Haugstad pointed out that fishermen's funds paid for many park improvements. He said South Branch Creek and Canfield Creek were the most important trout streams in Minnesota and the park was obliged to make improvements that would provide optimum fishing experiences for an increasing number of fishermen.

The MTA wanted restoration of work first done on South Branch Creek 29 years earlier and a new project on Canfield Creek to begin in 1999, with completion by October 1, 1999. The estimated cost was $100,000.

Representing Trout Unlimited, Tom Dornack also favored the project and felt that it would offer fishermen the larger size fish they needed to catch for an optimum fishing experience. He said his organization was working for the preservation of all plant and animal communities and that habitat improvement would increase in-stream biodiversity.

Forestville Administrator Mark White said the quality of Canfield Creek is due to geology, especially the presence of Big Spring, the source of the creek. The quality of the stream is also dependent on the state of the whole watershed, both in and out of the park.

He acknowledged the competing uses of the park: for camping, hiking, fishing, birding, horseback riding, and visits to historic sites and Mystery Cave. In the long run, he said, more of these interests would be served by promoting the overall health of the ecosystem and that the goal should be to work towards a pre-settlement arrangement.

Fisheries representative Mark Heywood said the department was looking at both watershed management and the management of individual streams. He said the South Branch Creek offered good trout numbers, but the sizes were small. Fisheries had planned a trout assessment for the spring, to be followed by a meeting with the Division of Parks in early summer, with the hope of making a decision by August 1, 1998.

District 31 State Senator Kenric J. Scheevel said the important thing was to produce trophy trout to keep fishermen coming to Southeast Minnesota. He said that habitat improvement would be good for all the wildlife, including birds.

The Chairman of the MOU Conservation Committee, Bob Holtz, pointed out that habitat improvement for trout degrades habitat for the endangered Louisiana waterthrush, a species known to nest along Canfield Creek. Holtz also suggested the management of people, instead of managing the environment for people.

The meeting ended with everyone agreeing that it was important to have this type of a meeting before work began, to avoid problems like those at Beaver Creek State Park, where the project began before the public was informed or consulted.

* * *

Forestville State Park, October, 2000

John Hockema, my good birding friend, guided Dana Gardner and me through Forestville State Park. It was a chilly day and Dana and I hadn't dressed warmly enough, but that didn't stop us.

At a bend in the trail, in a grassland area between Canfield Creek and us, we heard and saw a lot of bird activity. Some of the birds were common species that stay throughout the year. Most were white-throated sparrows on their way south. We also saw swamp and Lincoln's sparrows and a late common yellowthroat, a warbler species.

When we reached Canfield Creek, we immediately noticed riprapping (rock backfill) along the banks of the creek. John and Dana were surprised when I told them these rocks were covering oak planks that covered 4 x 5-foot lunker units used as sheltering places for brown trout. The big flat rocks rested neatly along the banks—too neatly.

As we walked, we found more birds. A belted kingfisher zoomed down the creek. A brown creeper crept up and around a tree trunk looking for insects. House and winter wrens fussed amongst the riprapping. Golden-crowned and ruby-crowned kinglets fluttered in the trees.

John told us he had done a study the summer before of Louisiana waterthrush and did not find any nesting pairs in the park.

Part II

Trout Opener – 1996

Once trout season opens, I am likely to encounter at least one fisherman whenever I walk along the South Fork. I like most of the fishermen I meet; they are quiet, they step gently and they usually walk alone. Sometimes we nod across the stream. Sometimes I ask what they're catching and they, noticing the binoculars around my neck, ask me what birds I'm seeing. The opening day of trout season is different—much busier.

The day before the 1996 trout season began, I stopped at the bridge over the South Fork. I leaned over the red iron railing and looked through the clear stream straight to the bottom where I could see the architecture of the stream's floor: small hills, valleys, rock out-croppings, fish hide-aways, forests of moss and trails of leaves, twigs and unknown entities.

Suddenly, I heard a loud voice on the Big Woods road where I could walk for hours without seeing anyone. A white Tri-County Electric truck with red letters on its side and a loudspeaker blaring messages from a CB radio approached the bridge. I waved to the driver. He waved back, then pulled over to the side of the road just past the bridge.

"Has the DNR stocked the stream yet?" he asked.

"I don't know," I said. "I haven't seen them."

"Well, they better do it soon. There'll be lots of people here tomorrow."

"Trout opener," I said. "Well, there are fish in there all right."

I left the Tri-County man leaning over the red iron railing and continued my walk. I found the native brook trout in the pool where I had been watching them for more than a year. The pool is in a hidden spot in a spring-fed brook with good cover: overhanging willows, basswood, brush, and shelves of rock.

I watched the trout hover in the water, their red fins swaying in a Paleozoic rhythm. I could see the white and black trim on their fins and white lines bordering their red bellies. I could see flashes of red under their gills, and red body spots against green and gold backgrounds that mimicked the bottom of the pool. As time went on, I saw more fish and wondered if they had been there all along.

On my way back home, I saw another car near the bridge. Two men climbed out. One stood over the red railing. One walked toward me.

Brown Trout

"Turkey tracks," he said, pointing to the road. "Do you ever see them around here?"

"Sometimes," I said, not telling him that I had just seen two Tom turkeys fanning their tails and strutting among eight grazing females.

"Turkey tracks!" he yelled to his partner.

"There are fish in here all right!" his partner yelled back.

I continued my walk home.

On opening day, I woke early and went to the bridge to watch the fishermen. I watched them bonding with their sons and daughters as they prepared their hooks and lines. I watched them cast their lines into the stream. I saw children running along the banks and heard them laughing and calling to each other. I saw mothers setting out picnic lunches.

I could hear my father's voice saying, "You have to be careful with trout. They can feel the vibration of your feet and, if it's a sunny day, they can see your shadow. I've caught some big browns and rainbows in this stream, but you have to know how to do it. The trout are wary. It takes a lot of skill to catch them."

I walked away from the bridge, smiling to myself.

Migration Survey

May 1998

Suddenly, I was face-down in mud. I didn't get up immediately; I couldn't believe I that I had tripped over debris left by spring flooding on the river bottoms. I could hear traffic roaring past on Highway 61, but it was not part of the world I was in—lying in Mississippi mud, with trees rising 60 feet over my head and red-winged blackbirds calling "konk-a-ree."

The reality of my situation finally sank into my brain. I got up, wiped off my face, brushed off my binoculars, retrieved my muddy field notes and moved on.

I was in the middle of my first point count for the U.S. Fish and Wildlife Service. Point counts are a systematic way to determine the presence of birds. The counter stands in a pre-determined spot and counts all the birds she sees and/or hears within 50 feet for a period of 10 minutes, then moves on to the next pre-determined area to do more of the same.

I could not allow much time for any particular bird. I had to make quick decisions about identifications and push my perfectionism to the background. It's a fine line between being sure and sure enough. If I was not sure enough, my instructions were to

*American Redstart
in Sugar Maple*

count the genus only. For example, an unidentified warbler would be recorded as "warbler species."

Suddenly, I realized I'd been hearing Tennessee warblers and not the chattering of house wrens. How could I have mistaken them? I had been concentrating so hard that a cardinal sounded like an exotic bird. I had to calm down. I could do this. After all, I passed the bird song test with a perfect score.

I had been studying bird songs for years, but never as systematically as I did in preparation for this work. Learning the common songs and their variations was important because it allowed me to rule out certain birds and then work on the more difficult ones. It was helpful to listen to different tape recordings of the same species, but recordings had their limitations. For me, studying songs from a tape was like trying to learn a foreign language in a classroom.

It was also helpful to learn the habits of particular species. A bird creeping up a tree trunk is probably a brown creeper. A bird creeping down a trunk is probably a nuthatch. A bird on the ground could be a thrush. If it pumps its tail, it's a hermit thrush. Habitat and time of day are also good indicators.

A robin sang. Now that's one bird I knew. Or maybe not. It could have been a scarlet tanager, which the field guides say sounds like a hoarse robin. A couple of tree swallows sounded like 50 birds. What I thought was a chestnut-sided warbler turned out to be a singing yellow warbler. A palm warbler sounded like a junco; a redstart could have been almost any bird.

When I arrived at the next counting point, I remembered my supervisor's words, "You were my first choice for this job. I wouldn't have picked you if I didn't think you could do it. If you go with your gut, you'll be okay."

I marked down a distant phoebe then felt unsure. A minute later, I heard it clearly. Confirmation. My confidence returned. Maybe I knew more than I thought I did.

After finishing my counts, I climbed back up out of the bottom-lands to Highway 61 and my parked car. I wondered if anyone in the traffic streaming by had noticed me and tried to figure out what a lone woman, covered with mud and carrying a bunch of loose papers and a pair of binoculars, was doing down there.

It took me longer to cross the mental space between the wild and civilized worlds than it took to cross the physical distance.

I got into my car and pulled off my waders, then quickly sorted through my scribbled papers to try to make sense out of my notes and charts before I forgot what I'd just experienced.

I still had five mixed woodlands sites to visit that day and would return to visit all of the sites seven more times before my work would be done.

Yellow-bellied Sapsucker

We met at the peanut butter log near my front door. We looked into each other's eyes, mine as big as his head, his eyes as big as the head of a pin.

It was April 1, 1999 and the yellow-bellied sapsucker had returned, announcing his arrival by drumming on the metal roof of our woodshed. I heard his plaintive squeal and watched him fly to his old nest hole in a nearby poplar tree. His short legs, strong claws and stiff tail held him in place.

He called again and latched onto another poplar, where he began to drill small holes. I could hear his steady tap-tap-tapping. The holes would become wells for sap, which he would lick with his long hairy tongue.

An insect attracted to the sweet liquid is a goner; this bird loves sap-soaked insects, which also give him a way to carry the sap to his young. Hummingbirds, warblers, kinglets and small mammals also drink from sapsucker wells, which can be found in more than 200 species of trees.

When the female sapsucker arrived on the scene, the drumming duets began. Other common displays include bill raising, crest raising, bowing, wing flicking and drooping, fluttering or undulating courtship flights, and ritual tapping at the nest entrance. The female looks like her partner, but lacks his red throat. Sapsuckers mate for life, which probably has more to do with site fidelity than love.

The male selects the nest site, usually in a live birch, aspen, or poplar affected by tinder fungus. Decaying wood inside the tree provides a soft nesting place, while the hard outer wood protects the young from predators. Both male and female excavate the nest hole. The female commonly lays five to six eggs, which hatch in 12-13 days. The female incubates and broods during the day, the male at night.

From April 25 to May 10, I observed the pair excavating their gourd-shaped nest hole. I first saw them carrying food to the nest on May 24. That's when the male began to fixate on the peanut butter.

For several years, I had been spreading peanut butter mixed with cornmeal on a log hanging from our feeder pole. Other birds gathered around when I filled the log, but were usually too timid to feed until I stepped away. Not the yellow-bellied sapsucker. The minute I arrived, he zoomed in and began to eat or gather food for his young.

He looked smaller and more vulnerable close up than far away. I could see his individual feathers, where the red on his throat merged with his black bib, the yellowish wash on his belly. His whole body could fit in my hand, but his personality and intensity rivaled mine. I wondered what he saw when he looked at me.

My friend flew back and forth from the feeder to the nest all day long. As far as I knew, the female never visited the feeder, although I saw her carrying food. By June 5, I could hear the nest-lings constantly and loudly begging. On June 9, they poked their heads out of the hole. Two days later, they were out of the nest.

Upon fledging, the parents teach their young the art of sapsucking. Alexander Skutch writes in *Parent Birds and Their Young* (1976) that the mother leaves the family four or five days after fledging has occurred. The father remains with his young for about two weeks.

I didn't see the birds again until the middle of July, when I heard tapping on an adolescent elm and found two juvenile sapsuckers working their holes. The last time I saw them before they flew south was October 2.

Yellow-bellied
Sapsucker

On April 6, 2000, I heard a loud drumming on the metal roof of our woodshed. The sapsucker's irregular drumming pattern distinguishes him from all other local woodpeckers.

My friend was six days late in his arrival; I was relieved to hear him. I watched him fly to a poplar tree where he began to drill small holes. Soon his mate would arrive and the cycle of reproduction would begin once more.

Bluff Country
Bird Festival

In May 2000, a group of participants in the Second Annual Bluff Country Bird Festival went on a field trip to DunRomin Park and Campground near Caledonia in Houston County. The field trip was led by Jaime Edwards, Minnesota Department of Natural Resources Nongame Wildlife Specialist, and me.

Soon after we arrived, a flurry of activity drew our eyes to a low branch in a maple tree. A closer look revealed a bump of grayish-green lichen about 1½ inches in diameter and 1½ inches high. Suddenly, a hummingbird whirred in and settled down in the bowl of a tiny nest to incubate two tiny eggs.

She had created this small wonder from plant down, fiber, bud scales and lichen; it was attached to the branch with spider silk. A close look showed the diminutive mother breathing. We were quite sure she saw us, but we couldn't imagine what we looked like to her.

As we watched the little hummer, Peter and Dawn Johnson, owners of the park, told us that the first owner, Don Anderson, an over-the-road trucker, had come upon the area 28 years earlier, fell in love with it, purchased the property and said he was "Done Roaming."

The park, with its wooded hillsides, open fields, a remote pond and a winding stream provides good habitat for songbirds. A hiking trail meanders through all of these habitats.

At the entrance to the trail, we heard the call of a tufted titmouse, an uncommon bird in Minnesota. An eastern wood-pewee sang a plaintive song while perched on a dead branch. Periodically, he flew out from the branch to grab an insect, then flew back to the same perch as though pulled by a string. A haunting wood thrush song came from deep in the woods and a great crested flycatcher boisterously and repeatedly called "wheep-wheep." We saw American redstarts, black and orange warblers about 4½ inches long, flitting through the trees singing squeaky songs.

Indigo buntings in iridescent blue breeding colors sang all morning long. Catbirds, rose-breasted grosbeaks and red-winged blackbirds were abundant. Red admiral butterflies were present by the hundreds, along with tiger swallowtails and hundreds of little white and yellow butterflies. In the creek, we saw a school of native brook trout.

The birders were able to identify a sharp-shinned hawk soaring overhead, thanks to the identification tips they had learned the night before from Scott Mehus, Flicker Ridge Naturalist from Buffalo City, Wisconsin.

In his presentation, Scott had said, "Stop and smell the roses and enjoy all the things you look at—turtles, trees, flowers, butterflies and birds. The neat thing about birds is that you can't ever know everything." Because ornithologists depend on observations from hobbyists, "birdwatching is really a citizen science," Scott had told us.

* * *

Chuck Juhnke, interpretive naturalist at Frontenac State Park and John Hockema, a Rochester bird enthusiast with an especially good ear for birdsongs, led a Festival field trip to Beaver Creek Valley State Park.

Participants crossed a swinging foot bridge over a crystal-clear creek filled with brilliant green watercress and other aquatic vegetation. Birds flew from tree to tree, back and forth across the creek. Their songs filled the air as watchers found the park's signature birds: Acadian flycatchers, cerulean warblers and Louisiana waterthrush—all protected species.

* * *

Ruby-throated Hummingbird

The wetland habitat of Mound Prairie Marsh and the LaCrescent Dump near the Mississippi River were the sites of another Saturday morning field trip. Participants in this trip found sandhill cranes, nesting black terns, great egrets, solitary sandpipers, great blue herons, green herons, possibly a little blue heron, a variety of ducks and other birds.

* * *

From 5:00 to 7:00 a.m., before the field trips and breakfast at the MaCalGrove Country Club, a group of early birders had searched for the elusive bobwhites. Although disappointed in their quest, they were treated to the sight of three red fox kits at play.

Saturday afternoon included a trip to view an active bald eagle nest; a wildflower hike in Beaver Creek State Park where columbine, Virginia waterleaf, Jack-in-the-pulpits, trillium, miterwort, buttercups and other flowers were blooming; and a birds of prey program at the Houston Nature Center presented by Alice, the great horned owl, and her human, Karla Kinstler.

Saturday evening featured a dinner at the MaCalGrove Country Club, where field trip leaders reported on their sightings and arrived at a tally of more than 100 bird species. Conversations were lively among the newly acquainted bird enthusiasts from all over Minnesota and parts of Wisconsin.

After dinner, some of the birders left for nearby Camp Winnebago where they stood before a spring gushing out of the earth, the water tumbling over rocks down to Winnebago Creek. Sheets of fog, soon to become dew, floated just above the ground.

From the foliage at the edge of the creek, a common yellowthroat sang its last concert of the day. In spite of John Hockema's efforts to rouse the bird, it refused to show itself.

Scarlet tanagers, cardinals, and robins sang in the distance. Nearby, a catbird reviewed its full repertoire of daytime songs.

Swallows swooped through the air, snapping up insects. Bats did the same. The birders had hoped to hear the call of a whip-poor-will, but none was to be heard.

As darkness deepened, the frog concert nearly drowned the other night sounds. Jaime Edwards, who had decided to give the group a lesson on frogs, almost fell into a pond trying to catch one. She finally caught an American toad and pointed out its large paired spots and warts, bulging eye ridges and its red, green and yellow colors.

Before many more hours, the first signs of Sunday morning would break through the darkness of night and a few intrepid birders would again be out in the field looking for the elusive bobwhite.

After another breakfast at MaCalGrove Country Club, the participants would take part in another round of field trips before heading home.

The Great Horned Owl of Houston

A visit to the area's newest nature center

A piercing shriek startled me; a red-winged blackbird flew so close that I could feel the rush of his wings. Naturalist Karla Kinstler told me that the blackbird was protecting his fledglings; he greeted everyone who came to the new Houston Nature Center (HNC) in the same manner. Houston (pronounced Hooston) is in the county of the same name.

The people of Houston had begun to make plans for a nature center when they learned that the Root River Trail would come through their town. At about the same time, the city needed to acquire 18 acres along the Root River to have its levee refurbished.

Fixing the levee resulted in the formation of a wetland near an existing small wetland. The town's people placed the nature center in this area and appointed Karla Kinstler as its naturalist.

Karla graduated from Luther College in Decorah, Iowa, in 1994 with a degree in biology. She became interested in nature as a young girl. While working on her family's farm not far from what would become the nature center, she noticed red-tailed hawks

Great Horned Owl

following her to grab up the small rodents she exposed while raking hay. The hawks sparked her interest in birds of prey.

After college, she worked at Forestville State Park. I met her there when I attended her talk on falconry, during which she displayed Duncan, an American kestrel, North America's smallest falcon. She no longer has Duncan; one day while he was free-flying, two other kestrels chased him away and she never saw him again.

In 1998, Karla acquired Alice, a great horned owl. When Alice was a nestling, someone shot her father, brother and mother and Alice fell out of her nest, permanently damaging a wing. Her brother and father died of their injuries.

Marge Gibson, a soft-hearted bird rehabilitator in Antigo, Wisconsin, brought Alice back to health. Alice's mother also survived her injuries and is now a teaching bird, like her daughter.

Because she is imprinted on humans and can only fly short distances, Alice can not survive in the wild. She lives with Karla and her husband, Ken, in their home in Houston. Although she has a room of her own, she flies around the house at will. She has a favorite window from which she watches birds. Her favorite place to sleep is on top of a bookcase. She has a favorite blanket that she pounces on and attacks.

To satisfy her preening instinct in the absence of other owls, Alice preens Ken and Karla, working through their hair and nibbling their ears. They, of course, must return the favor. She makes soft noises for attention, responds to hugs by ruffling or rousing her feathers and screeches when her humans are gone too long.

As I visited with Karla, Alice sat in her mews (a large open-air cage) watching birds. The mews was near a small Sno-cone hut that served as the HNC's temporary headquarters. Karla showed me the plans for a permanent building that would consist of a lobby, offices, a display area and an interpretive area.

At the entrance to the temporary building was a large sign with the Center's logo, which incorporates the name of the center with the abstract face of a great horned owl. Inside, displays and specimens, most of which Karla had prepared herself, covered several tables and the walls.

While at Luther College, Karla worked as a museum assistant for Tex Sordahl, resident ornithologist and biology professor. From

Professor Sordahl, she learned how to prepare and catalog bones, feathers, body parts and skins.

Karla showed me how she had tagged each specimen according to accepted standards and had cataloged it in phylogenetic and numerical order. In the past, specimens were collected by killing birds and other creatures. This is no longer the case. Specimens are acquired now only when animals die from accidents or old age.

I had a few moments alone to look at Karla's displays when builder and volunteer Wayne Dosch arrived to deliver an outdoor bulletin board. In a corner, I found prairie seed packets; above the desk, a display of field guides; and hanging from the ceiling, t-shirts and sweatshirts printed with HNC's logo.

On one table, I found woodpecker wings, heads, bills, tails, feet and tongues, along with careful descriptions and labels. On other tables were the equivalent body parts of birds of prey, along with samples of owl pellets, fossils, the skin of a fawn and skulls of coyotes, raccoons and squirrels. The skin of a timber rattler hung in a long transparent tube on the back wall.

When I went outside to take a photograph of Wayne and Karla unloading the bulletin board, I found that it was raining. We'd already had too much rain, which had resulted in the flooding of roads, trails, fields and some houses.

Due to the flooding, three sections of blacktop on the Root River Trail from Money Creek Woods to Houston had disappeared, making it necessary to close the trail. By the time this new rain stopped, two more inches had fallen.

Before leaving the nature center, I walked over to look once more into the penetrating eyes of Alice, the great horned owl.

A Small World

May 30: My day began with a walk to the silver nest in the branches of a young elm. When I approached, the little redstart sang his piercing song. His mate flew to the nest, looked inside, then settled down on top of it.

When I turned to look out across the field, I saw the bluebirds carrying grubs into their house, then flying back out carrying little white sacks.

A low trilling sound coincided with a pair of cardinals flying to a nest in a blue spruce. When I looked into the nest, I saw three downy creatures crying for food.

June 5: I told my husband about the cardinal nest and the three tiny nestlings. He looked, but found no babies, only one small bluish spotted egg.

I took him to see the redstart nest, now a skeleton of its former self, bits of grass and thatch caught here and there along the trunk of the tree.

As the day went on, we heard the bluebird insistently calling. Her mate flew from the nest to an old oak tree, back and forth, back and forth. We saw two fledglings on the ground, begging for food. The father returned to the nest again. Hey Dad! They've flown the coop!

It was a big day here in the woods—a small world to us; all of existence to the baby birds. But soon they would fly south and their world would grow larger than ours.

June 7: I found one bluish egg cracked open on the ground near the blue spruce. I saw the female cardinal gathering nesting material.

*Eastern
Bluebird on
Mullein Stalk*

New Life

Young cottontails play leap frog in the grass while a hummingbird performs a mating dance.

A red-bellied woodpecker whines for food from his parents. When they don't come, he feeds himself.

Pileated woodpecker parents take turns trying to satisfy the hunger of their huge babies, who teeter on the edge of their nest hole gathering courage for their first flights.

Twin fawns mimic their mother as she stomps her foot to warn of danger.

An oriole dive-bombs a squirrel who comes too close to his nest. A ruffed grouse whimpers and plays the broken wing trick as her babies go peeping and scurrying through the underbrush.

In the night, a young raccoon watches the cats on their porch as they watch him. Then he ambles to the bird feeder where he meticulously picks out dropped sunflower seeds, takes them to the birdbath and washes them with little pink fingers until they are soft enough to eat.

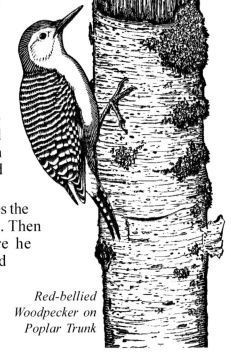

Red-bellied Woodpecker on Poplar Trunk

Survival

Beaver Creek State Park

Beaver Creek was crystal clear and studded with watercress. Dana Gardner and I walked along the shores of this winding jewel in search of birds. An Acadian flycatcher, the first ever for Dana, performed perfectly. A cerulean warbler, another first, sang from the tree tops. A veery and a black-billed cuckoo sang from deep in the woods. Bird song surrounded us; the temperature was right and the sky was partly blue. Suddenly, it became dark, as if someone had turned out the lights. Rain began to fall.

It was still raining when I arrived back home in the Big Woods. By the time the storm ended some time in the night, the rainfall totaled five inches for the second time in two weeks.

On my walk the next morning, I discovered the rain had carved deep ruts into our driveway and destroyed a culvert on our township road. I gingerly picked my way along the slivers of remaining road.

Tree trunks littered the road and the South Fork was over its banks. Trout swam in the ditches. I thought about the birds. How many nests were destroyed? How many birds died? Was Beaver Creek as muddy and angry as the South Fork? I thought about other storms. One in particular stood out.

* * *

It was a late afternoon in July 1997. Lightning flashed. Rain and wind pummeled the woods. Suddenly, we heard a crash that wasn't thunder; a giant white oak had fallen into our yard. The next day, when we began to cut the tree for firewood, we counted 220 growth rings. We realized the tree must have been a sapling in Thomas Jefferson's time, supple then, twisting in the wind, its survival uncertain.

In the 1980s, when we were still supple, we had heated our house entirely with wood that we cut ourselves. I remember aching backs, sawdust covering us from head to toe and slashes in Art's jeans from the chainsaw blade that barely missed his knees. Back then, the trees we cut didn't fall neatly into our yard. When the branches tripped Art, he blamed me for not pulling them away soon enough. I cried and blamed him for expecting too much. His rolling eyes said, "Just like a woman."

By the time we cut into the fallen giant white oak in 1997, our marriage had matured. I saw Art stumble over a branch without saying a word, without rolling his eyes. I didn't cry or blame him for expecting too much.

The giant tree was leaning against a young white pine, bending the pine to a 45-degree angle. We wanted to save the young tree, so Art pushed a chain under the oak while I climbed through prickly ash to the other side, reached underneath, grabbed a thistle, found the end of the chain and wrapped it around the trunk. When Art started the tractor and waited for me to climb out of the way, I felt proud of our skill, the way we made things work and the way we held our tongues.

The wood we cut from the oak had almost filled our shed. Three years later, the shed still held enough wood for a couple of hard winters. The last 10 feet of the oak's trunk, too thick for the chainsaw blade, still sat at the edge of our yard. We pointed it out to Dana and some of his Lanesboro friends who had come to see the woods and watch for birds. The young pine hadn't survived.

As we sat visiting on our porch, we noted woodpeckers, chickadees and titmice coming to the feeders. We listened to the songs of rose-breasted grosbeaks, indigo buntings and red-eyed vireos. We watched redstarts flit about in the trees. We pointed out the hairy woodpecker hole from which the baby birds had recently fledged.

We didn't tell our guests about the fledgling that flew into a window and died. I didn't tell our guests about the trout swimming

*Downy Woodpecker
in White Oak*

in the ditches, or the toad I tried to nudge off the road to safety after the first big rain and how it had hopped away on three legs, its fourth leg dragging uselessly across the gravel.

As we talked, I saw us through our visitors' eyes and realized how much we belong to the woods. We are part of the woods, not merely living in it. We are in the rhythm of its seasons. We empathize with parent birds' anxiety for newly fledged babies and feel relief when the babies survive.

We empathize with other survivors also: the deer with an injured leg and the raccoon that walked on three legs and had a stump of a tail. We are survivors too—of aching backs, chainsaw threats, tears, blame, wind and rain.

We feel proud of our skill, the way we make things work and the way we speak without words.

A Big Woods Wedding

A medieval scene greeted guests as they walked down green paths through open woods and across hilly fields to a small white tent with open walls. The groom could have been Robin Hood, complete with his Merry Men, anxiously waiting for his bride to appear—tall, slender and beautiful like Maid Marian.

In this setting, Sandra Albro, daughter of Corina and Greg Albro of Elkton, Oregon, married Brandon Rutter, son of Mary Lewis of Decorah, Iowa and Phil Rutter of Canton, Minnesota. The wedding site was on land at Brandon's boyhood home, the Badgersett Research Farm, in our own Big Woods.

The bride and groom had met at Swarthmore College in Swarthmore, Pennsylvania, where they both received under-graduate degrees. The Merry Men, including Brandon, made up an eight-member singing group from Swarthmore officially known as the Sixteen Feet. The group had existed for many years, with new members joining as others graduated. They sang a cappella in the Do-wop style, using their own voices as accompaniment, instead of musical instruments. Their first music for the wedding was "Pachobel's Canon."

As part of the ceremony, friends and relatives stood to speak
for the couple. Emotions run deep at a wedding. Some of the guests
shed a few tears. Sandra touched her eyes from time to time with
an embroidered handkerchief that was a gift from her dad—an
unusual gift, she had said and the best thing he could have given
her for this day.

Mary, Brandon's mom, had spent a lot of time rehearsing
the poem she had written for the couple, so that she would not
cry while delivering it. Even so, her voice broke at the end,
when she said:

> "Cast your eyes through a tunnel of trees that twists
>   beyond your sight too soon.
> Imagine rocky hills and sunny glens, the murky
>   tumble of day on day.
> Ponder the long road in all its fervent brevity.
> Hold fast the singular beauty of the moment that
>   passes but lives always.

Common Yellowthroat

Celebrate the look in my son's eyes when he gazes
upon his beloved.

See the tenderness of her touch along his arm.

Find in their laughter a song as old as the earth and
as new as this day.

Embrace them with your hopes, for they have found
each other."

After saying their vows, the newlyweds walked arm in arm through the tent and down the green path, while the Sixteen Feet sang "An die Freude" ("Ode to Joy"), from Beethoven's Ninth symphony.

The reception took place in a wooded hollow. As guests approached the site, they saw two large open-walled tents with long tables stretching from side to side. Torches burned on the periphery of the hollow. Someone broke out the mead (actually, beer) and sparkling cider. This medieval feast came complete with a roast pig, dark bread and, as a concession to modern times, pasta salad and cut vegetables.

Perry, Brandon's brother and best man stood to give a toast. This was a moment for recollection. The memory that popped into my mind was of Mary skiing from Badgersett Farm to my house with Perry, barely a toddler, on her back and Brandon confidently skiing just behind.

One of the Sixteen Feet rose to give a toast. He talked about Sandra and Brandon's tender love for each other. He talked about the camaraderie of the singing group and told us that Brandon had always been the sensible one, the one who kept them grounded.

The time came for the bride and groom to cut their wedding cake, which had been made by Amish girls who were also present at the reception. While the cake was being served and eaten, the guests engaged in lively conversations.

Suddenly, all talking stopped as the Sixteen Feet, including Brandon, geared up to sing. Their voices and actions were meticulously coordinated. Everyone seemed instinctively to know what to do and when to do it. At the same time, they gave the feeling that it was all improvised.

Throughout the reception, another sort of music played itself out in the gentle evening songs of yellow warblers, common yellowthroats, chipping sparrows, song sparrows, red-winged blackbirds, bobolinks, American toads and tree frogs.

The celebration continued late into the night. When Mary said goodbye at 11:30 p.m., only the Sixteen Feet remained. One of the young men thanked Mary for having Brandon.

Sometime in the night, the newly weds rode off in a car—not on a steed—to begin their honeymoon.

Bird Survey
at Hvoslef WMA

Clint and Mabe Vickerman once lived on the edge of a field in what is now part of the Hvoslef Wildlife Management Area (WMA). Their two-story log house no longer exists. The old barn is gone, too. The big Chinese elms in their yard have become snags. I saw the Department of Natural Resources (DNR) people cutting them down to make room for native species.

In the 1950s, Preston resident and politician Moppy Anderson had bought the place and the surrounding property. He and his family had built a cabin close to the South Fork of the Root River, just down the hill from Clint and Mabe. The Andersons had allowed Clint and Mabe to stay in their house rent-free.

* * *

One summer morning, I found the brush pile of sawed-up Chinese elms alive with birds. It appeared that chickadees, wrens, indigo buntings and four species of sparrows had decided that the pile made a perfect place to park their children.

The sun was rising above the horizon. It was a glorious day, a welcome reprieve from a long humid bug-filled heat wave. A sedge wren flew from branch to branch, to within two feet of my face, where it stopped and sang its full repertoire of songs. The songs were wren-like, but more delicate than those of a house wren. As he sang, the pugnacious little bird seemed to look me right in the eye.

I was there to do a set of weekly point counts for a bird survey commissioned by the DNR. After completing a count at the old farm site, I walked east through the grassland. Along the edge of the woods, at a grove of red cedar trees, I found gray catbirds, rose-breasted grosbeaks, blue-gray gnatcatchers, a family of common yellowthroats, a family of field sparrows, and a mother song sparrow frantically jabbing food down the throats of her three wing-quivering young.

Continuing through grasslands along the edge of the woods, I went around to the south where I could hear the South Fork flowing below bluffs to my left. Soon I reached the old farm pond. A snapping turtle swam in the pond; cedar waxwings flew over the water snapping insects out of the air and a solitary sandpiper bobbed along the banks, methodically poking its bill into the mud.

South of the pond, I stopped for another count, then slowly made my way through the grassland and up the hill to the parking lot. Bobolinks and red-winged blackbirds were plentiful. I also found meadowlarks, dickcissels and a noisy family of eastern kingbirds. A great blue heron flew overhead.

Next, I walked east on the road back to Clint and Mabe's old place, then down a steep hill to Moppy's cabin site and the South

Wood Duck

Fork bottomlands. This area was good for chickadees, vireos, warblers, pewees and wrens.

At my final stop, where the road curves around Lawrence Simley's old farm, a wood thrush called from across the valley. Swallows, robins, song sparrows and yellow warblers were everywhere. I lingered, reluctant to leave this world and return to everyday life.

Eastern Kingbird in Black Locust

Green Lea Manor

Marjorie, a former nurse, walked around the front lobby, smoothing lap robes and feeling for pulses. Dora, a former receptionist, sat at the nursing station, rearranging papers and pens. Ingrid walked up and down the hallways in high heels and a Sunday dress. She nodded to those she passed and stopped at the nursing station to talk with Dora. I knew what they were talking about by their gestures, rhythm of speech and tones of voice, even though their words, garbled by Alzheimer's, were impossible to decipher.

"Amazing Grace" could be heard coming from the piano in the activity room. The pianist was 93-year-old Jessie.

Thor, who had recently celebrated his 100th birthday, complained, "I think my brain is trying to drive me crazy."

I heard Alveda and Dagmar reminiscing about the swing that used to hang from a branch in Alveda's yard.

Henrietta's great-granddaughter had just arrived with her new baby. Residents gathered to admire the tiny child.

Ethel, back from her walk to Margie's Sunshine Café, wandered into the front lobby. She smelled of smoke, which meant she had either begged a cigarette on the street or picked a butt out of the ditch. When I asked where she had gotten the cigarette, she shook her fist at me and stomped off to her room.

I had just finished setting up my 3:00 p.m. medications and was about to make my first rounds of the evening shift at Green Lea Manor, a nursing home in the small town of Mabel, where no one

*Immature Robin
in American Elm*

is a stranger. I was the only R.N. on duty; therefore, I was in charge of the whole house—the LPNs, the nursing assistants and all 79 residents. This responsibility would have been daunting without the skill and competence of my co-workers.

I began my rounds with four women who were playing canasta at a table near the front window. I gave the women their medications and visited a little about the weather. When I moved on to Clara, who was sitting nearby in her wheelchair, I overheard the canasta players talking about me.

"She's a nice nurse, isn't she?" Irma said. "She and her man came from the Twin Cities. They built a house in the Big Woods, you know."

Lydia said, "Too many crazy people out there—shoot you soon as look at you."

Clara, who raised her family 70 years ago on the small woodland farm bordering our property, had often told me stories about the Big Woods. She talked of its Ozarks-like quality, the squatters, the incest and how everyone used to watch out for each other; they were like a big family.

Belle was also part of the Big Woods family. I found her sitting in her wheelchair watching exotic birds in a cage.

She talked about her home: "I have to get home and take care of things. Have you checked on my house? Are the windows broken? Is the porch falling off?"

I told her I had seen a couple of broken windows, but the porch had looked okay. Until recently, Belle and her brother Lawrence had lived in the house where they were born on the farm their parents homesteaded more than 100 years earlier.

When Lawrence broke his arm and became disoriented, their nephew brought him here to Green Lea Manor. The family then decided Belle shouldn't live alone; they had to remove her from her home by force.

When I left Belle to visit the rooms in the south hallway, I met Lawrence. "How are you today?" I asked. He smiled his shy smile and gave his usual reply: "I'm just fine. I never smoked or drank and I never had any stomach trouble."

Continuing down the south hallway, I stopped to redirect Harold, who was pinching the bottom of every nursing assistant he passed. I noticed Sylvia coughing on her way to the smoking porch, where Harry sat in his fireproof vest, a lit cigarette balanced between two yellow fingers. Annette, one of the nursing assistants, kept an eye on him so he wouldn't burn the place down.

I stopped to greet 92-year-old Stella, who was moving from room to room, visiting old neighbors and friends.

Nels' daughter Corinne, who was just leaving, told me her father was having a good day. I found Nels sitting in his wheelchair, watching birds at the feeder outside his window.

"Look at that robin," he said. "I think she has a nest in one of those bushes."

I found Alice in her room, visiting with her daughter and little dog, the only two beings she recognized. Her daughter tried to convince her that the pills I wanted her to take were not poisoned.

When I entered Larry's room to check his blood sugar, he showed me his World War II combat scars. When I changed the dressing on Henry's arm, he showed me pictures of Canton, his hometown, taken when he was a boy in 1908.

Excitement was brewing nearby. "There's a bride here," someone said. It was Helen's granddaughter, Sarah, and her new husband, still dressed in their wedding clothes. The look on Helen's face revealed the importance of this visit.

Next door, family members hovered over the bed of a 50-year-old hospice patient who was dying of breast cancer. In a barely audible voice, Lorna, the patient, asked for water. Family members jumped to help, to do something besides wait.

Soon Lorna would stop speaking. She had already stopped eating. Her breathing would become slower and more irregular. Then she would stop breathing and her family would begin to cry. She'd breathe again and her children would resume their waiting positions, dry-eyed. This would go on for hours before Lorna finally took her last breath.

I saw Liz, one of the nursing assistants, coming down the hallway with coffee and cookies for the family.

So far, the shift was running smoothly. For this, I could thank the nursing assistants, Sally, Gail, Kathy, Annette, Liz and Tammy. Although I was the charge nurse, it was the nursing assistants who determined how well the shift would run. They spent more time with the residents than anyone. If they were brusque and impatient, the residents were discontented and anxious. If they were patient and gentle, a feeling of calmness would spread throughout the house.

After supper, I found Ed calmly showing Sally the pictures in his photo album. I knew Sally was busy and I appreciated the time she was taking with Ed, who was otherwise confused and disruptive. Next door, Gail helped her grandmother, Ruth, prepare for bed. Liz gently turned Angie's arthritic pretzel-like body, rubbed her with lotion and placed pillows behind her back and between her knees, to protect her from bedsores.

Back at the nurse's station, Annette told me that Beatrice was ready for her Tylenol, Clara would like a Darvocet for leg pain, and Arden needed some Milk of Magnesia. After delivering these medications, I prepared supplies and medication for Ray's peritoneal dialysis, which did the work of his kidneys through a fluid exchange in his abdomen.

Ray was here, temporarily, due to weakness from an infection. Normally he did his dialysis at home, where he used devices of his own creation to make the task easier. Ray didn't want to talk about his illness. We talked instead about farming. He showed me a picture of his farm, taken from an airplane window.

Gail poked her head in the door to report another break in Olga's paper-thin skin. I noticed blood on Gail's arm. "It's where Olga scratched me," she said.

Olga was frightened of us, I thought, and that was why she was combative. I could only imagine what her world was like inside her Alzheimer's-ravaged brain.

While I was cleaning and dressing Olga's wound, Tammy came to report a reddened area on Wilbur's coccyx. I noticed a welt on Tammy's arm. She said it was where Wilbur pinched her when she tried to clean him after a toilet accident.

* * *

Most of the residents in Green Lea Manor had been hard-working, productive people all of their lives and were accustomed to being self-sufficient. It was frustrating and embarrassing for them to have to depend on others for help with even the most intimate of bodily functions.

It is up to the nursing assistants to meet these needs efficiently, while preserving privacy and dignity. Only certain people can do this job well. And yet, the brunt of nursing home criticisms are often leveled at these most valuable and low-paid individuals.

Nursing homes receive a lot of criticism. It is difficult to avoid the institutional feel of nursing homes, especially the larger ones. And, there is always the potential for the abuse of vulnerable older adults who are too incapacitated to complain. Understaffing (to cut costs or as a result of worker shortages) often results in slow responses to call lights and the necessity of rushing residents through daily activities such as bathing, dressing and eating. The physical and mental incapacities of residents and their grief over their loss of independence also can potentially contribute to an unhappy atmosphere.

Green Lea Manor does not fit the institutional stereotype. Residents here often retain their place in the community. Everyone has visitors. Relatives, friends and old neighbors frequently come to see more than one person and often take the time to introduce themselves to those they don't know. The Midwestern work ethic is strong here; most caregivers cannot conceive of doing a bad job. Most have relatives here, which ensures kindness and compassion. Who would mistreat a grandmother, an uncle, or an old friend?

* * *

The evening shift was nearly over. Nursing assistants were finishing last rounds, carrying soiled linens to the laundry chute and answering call lights.

Someone gently stopped Sydna from wheeling herself out the door when she said she needed to go get her mail. Dora, in tears, paced back and forth in front of the windows, trying to embrace her own reflection. Annette took her by the hand and walked her to her room.

The night staff had arrived.

On my way out the front door, I said goodnight to Thor, who couldn't sleep and was still up, playing solitaire in the front lobby.

Stella

She wore her dignity like a Sunday dress as she moved from room to room, visiting old neighbors and friends. She might have been strolling down the street, stopping to talk with neighbors on porches and front steps. She lent a sense of normalcy to the nursing home full of aging minds and failing bodies. She was proper, but not prim. At 92, Stella had returned to Mabel, the town of her birth, after many years of absence.

I was not surprised to learn that she was a retired teacher, but I was surprised to learn that she had taught in my hometown, 100 miles away. When I told her that Faribault was my hometown, she asked the familiar question, "Who are you, then?"

"My name is Nancy Overcott," I said. "My maiden name is Hielsberg"

"Oh, You're John's daughter, then. I remember John. He taught woodworking in the high school. Is he still alive?"

"No. He died five years ago, six years after my mother," I said.

Stella told me she had taught school in Faribault from 1950 to 1968. We reminisced about the schools and people we knew in common. She had taught in old Central, a large red brick school where I had gone to kindergarten. When they demolished Central, she went to McKinley.

After kindergarten, I had gone to Washington school. She said she knew my first and third grade teachers, Miss Bengston and Miss Mademann.

Stella talked about her friend and long-time roommate, Frances Wassman, also a teacher. She said they had traveled all over the country together. They remained roommates until recently, when Frances had become ill and had to move to a nursing home. Only then did they go their separate ways.

Later in the shift, I heard Stella talking with other residents, including her sister Mildred. "There's a nurse here who used to live in Faribault," she said. "She's John Hielsberg's girl." Of course, no one in the Manor knew who John Hielsberg was.

Stella began her teaching career in Canton in 1923, after receiving a two-year degree from Winona State Teacher's College. That's when she bought her first car, a Ford with a rumble seat. She said her students loved to ride in the car with her.

She also taught in Amherst, which was called String Town back then. Amherst, 15 miles northwest of Mabel on Fillmore County Road 23, barely exists now—except for the legendary Lily Haagenson's country store.

Stella also taught in Newburg, eight miles northwest of Mabel on County Road 24. Newburg is much smaller than it used to be. Its country store is no longer in business and hasn't been for years.

At present, the town consists of about a dozen houses, a sawmill, and the United Methodist Church, which was founded in 1860 and is now a historical landmark. The school no longer exists, except for bits of its foundation.

From Stella, I learned about the school as it once was—a two story brick building that contained two classrooms, a large dining hall and a gymnasium. All of its floors were white oak.

My co-worker Jackie told me that her father, who used to run the Newburg store, had wanted to buy the school and turn it into apartments, but Milton Gerard had bought it first and used it as part of his sawmill.

Stella also taught in Prosper, an unincorporated settlement on the Iowa border, three miles west of Mabel. Lanesboro resident Edna Thompson remembered Stella from that time: "She was one of the most influential people in my life. At 18 years of age, I was a student teacher under her at the Prosper two-room school. I'm sure my 37 years of teaching can be attributed to her mentoring. The Prosper school is a supper club now. You would never know it was once a school."

Stella's first four teaching jobs paid $40.00 a month. She recalled her interview in 1950 for the job in Faribault, a job with better pay.

"Do you remember Mr. Cross?" she asked. "He was the superintendent then. When he interviewed me, he asked if I would be willing to get my four-year degree. I said I would and he said, 'You've got the job.' So I started teaching in Faribault and went back to Winona in the summers to get my degree."

Soon after Stella arrived in the nursing home, her friend Frances died. Every day afterward, she asked me if I knew her friend. Every day I had to say no.

When I get old, I would like to be like Stella, a little forgetful, but with long-term memories intact. I would like to be as pleasant and dignified as she is, but I don't think I will be and I don't think I will return to the town of my birth, as she did. Faribault no longer holds much interest for me. I've put roots down in the Big Woods now, where I feel more at home than anywhere else.

A House Burning in the Big Woods

June 21: the Summer Solstice, the longest day of the year—in Pagan times, a day of magic, celebration and ritual dancing around fires.

* * *

A puff of smoke came from an upstairs window; it could have been from a cigarette, but we knew it wasn't. The Canton Fire Department was setting fire to the old Simley house. The firemen stood ready with their hoses to control the blaze. Suddenly, the house lit up from the inside.

We stepped back to get away from the heat. As the power of the fire asserted itself, human control seemed to hang by a thread. The firemen and their families, the new owners, neighbors and friends were there to bear witness; to experience the excitement and fear generated by a burning house.

Patrick and Lisa Luetmer of Rochester were the new owners of the Simley farm. At first, they thought they would save the century-old house in which Lawrence Simley and his sister Belle Olson were born, but the house had proved to be beyond repair.

As I watched the fire spread, I thought of Lawrence and Belle and wondered what it was like for them growing up there. I imagined Lawrence helping his father with farming chores and Belle helping her mother cook and preserve in their summer kitchen. I could see Belle sitting on her porch, shelling peas while looking down across a field to Simley Creek—also known as the South Fork of the Root River.

A deer bounded across the field. A red-tailed hawk soared overhead.

* * *

About ten years earlier, while walking along the creek upstream from my land, I had stopped to look into the fast-moving water. Before long, a reflection appeared next to mine.

I saw a shy smile and heard a soft voice with a Norwegian accent. "How are you today?" Lawrence Simley had asked. "Are you watching trout?"

We talked about his farm, its setting in the woods overlooking the stream, the bluffs rising on the other side and the wildlife he often saw.

He said, "My nephew thinks I'm too old to run this place. He says I should sell and move into town, but I don't want to leave the woods. Who will take care of the trees when I'm gone?"

The fire ate deeper into the house. Boards fell away, leaving the shape of a cross. The porch with its gingerbread trim went next. The upstairs window openings looked like the eyes of a Jack-o-lantern, until the fire lengthened and shaped them like the stained glass windows of a church. The fire extended to the summer kitchen. A huge cloud of black smoke billowed from a window. A burning shingle swirled into the air.

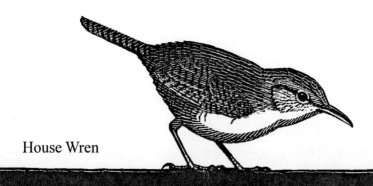

House Wren

A fireman directed his hose to a large spreading oak, older than the house. Lawrence would be pleased that this tree had been saved. The barn, built in 1936, would also be spared. It had a stone foundation and walls made of sturdy white pine.

Under the watchful eyes of their mothers, children played on the periphery of this burning. A house wren and a Baltimore oriole sang nearby. They had children, too.

As the house and summer kitchen became memories, it was obvious that the Canton firemen knew what they were doing. Perhaps their control over Mother Nature was never in question. Perhaps our fear was only our wish to experience fear.

Someone prepared a grill for the promised picnic. A flame from the grill licked at the bratwurst and hamburgers. Beer and pop came out of coolers. Patrick made a toast to Lawrence, Belle and their father, Thor. It was the end of an era—or was it?

* * *

The farm will always be called the Simley Place. The new owners are taking care of the trees and the trout will continue to swim in Simley Creek.

Storm
June 27, 1998

The six o'clock news showed a line of storms near Albert Lea, moving northeast. We were east of the storms. It looked like they would miss us, but we didn't turn off the television.

Then came a tornado warning for Rochester. We pitied the people in its path. The luxury of pity.

Thunder began to rumble. The sky was a non-menacing gray; we could see only part of it because of the tall trees that surrounded us.

Doppler images showed the storm ballooning with highest winds and tornadoes to the north, baseball-size hail in Austin on its way to Fillmore County. It was not going to miss us.

We decided to put the Buick in the open, so a tree wouldn't fall on it. We thought we would be okay. Our hills would break up the storms. We say this all the time.

Obsessed with the car, Art changed his mind and moved it under a tree to protect it from hail.

The storm began to hit Rochester with 80-mile an hour winds and driving rain. We listened to the sirens on the television. We never hear them here in the woods.

A warning for Fillmore County—for Harmony, 12 miles east, and Preston 15 miles northeast. It was hot, humid, no wind. No rain.

The week before, during another storm, we had huddled in the basement of our neighbor's barn because we have no basement ourselves.

Still thinking about our cars, Art yelled, "Get in the Subaru. Drive ahead of me down the driveway. We'll leave the Buick part way down in the shelter of the hill and take the Subaru to Bratrud's barn."

I stuffed computer disks, my daughters' pictures, a bond, his wallet, clean underwear and toothpaste into my purse. I threw food into the cats' bowls and unplugged the telephone, television and computers. I threw jackets, my purse and the weather radio into the Buick.

It began raining. The rain is a good sign. We always say this.

I suddenly realized I should have put my things in the Subaru, not the Buick.

"Who cares about stuff?" Art yelled. I retrieved the stuff anyway.

We drove to Bratrud's, parked near the barn and watched. The weather didn't look so bad, we thought. But then the rain intensified. We rolled the windows up. It was so hot!

"I'm going home," I cried. "I don't care if my house blows down around me. It's the only place I want to be."

Halfway up our driveway, we met the parked Buick. We didn't have time to move it. We would have to walk the rest of the way.

"I'm staying here," Art said.

I ran alone toward our house, which was visible in flashes of light. Wind whistled along the power lines, as it does through the rigging of our sailboat. I had never heard it like this on land before. Trees bowed at their waists.

Soaking wet and shaking, I leaned on the door, closing it against the wind. I checked for the cats. Max wove around my legs meowing. Limpy was under the bed, Nick under the couch.

The weatherman had said to stay away from open windows. But it was so hot and hard to breathe. I opened a window and let the rain come in. It felt cool. A branch sailed past. The cottonwood split in front of my eyes, just missing the house.

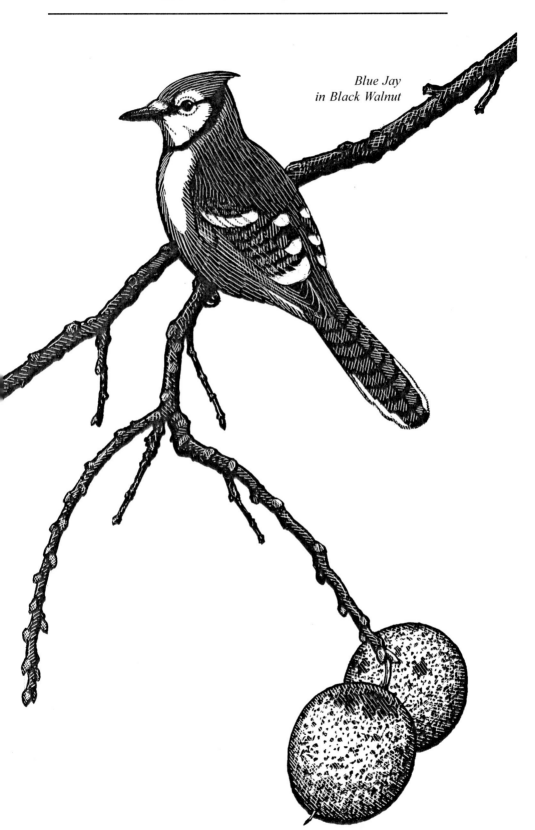

*Blue Jay
in Black Walnut*

The lights flickered off—on—off. I fumbled in the dark for a match and a cigarette. So much for quitting smoking. I made my way to the storeroom for candles and the kerosene lantern. What was happening out there? The wind let up.

The door opened. There stood Art, dripping wet.

Sometime in the night, there was another storm.

* * *

By the next morning, the electricity was on again. It was cool and clear. A gentle breeze was blowing. The birds were active and calling—frantically, it seemed. A robin's nest lay on the ground. Around it, I found little pieces of blue eggshells. The South Fork was brown and swollen. A willow had fallen across the bridge. I heard the neighbors' chainsaws roaring.

Winona County would have no power for 24 hours. Austin residents would have to wait a week. Austin lost 3,000 trees. A husband and wife camping at Shades of Sherwood Campground on the Zumbro River tried to go home in the midst of the storm. The Zumbro washed them off the road. Both drowned.

The Salvation Army was requesting bottled water, sandwich meat, batteries and generators.

Eulogy

The first bones belonged to a
   cow and her baby.

I collected them
in a pile by the river
a song sparrow sang

so I took them home:
   vertebrae, tibiae, fibulae,
jaws, clavicles, a pelvis
   under my arm
   (these last two
   were my
   favorites)

until greed took me
   searching in the
   bluffs

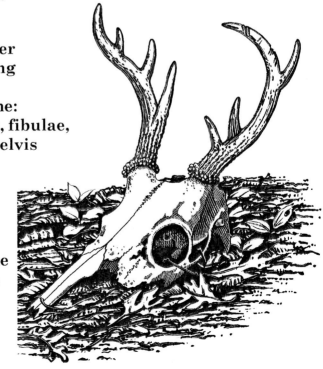

around coyote dens and intersections:
tiny indigestible mandibles,
coyote skulls, horns,
a fur-covered leg,
a hoof

after awhile
legs, ribs, and arms bored me unless they were small
as pins

when summer came they hid
under the carpet

I was grateful—

the obligation to clean, identify, display, honor,
turn this way and that was more
than I was prepared to devote my life to

so yesterday I kept the mandibles, skulls, two
    pelvises,
a couple clavicles
(organized the tiny bones in plastic trays)

returned the rest and wondered if
    what I left
near the salt lick would scare the
        deer.

Last night coyotes
howled under my
kitchen window.

Coyote

Butterflies
through Binoculars

In my back yard, I watched a small silent creature fluttering among the tall weeds—a creature that does not bite, sting or carry disease. It was bright orange, with dark bands on its upper parts and silver spots below. It is common in meadows, fields and along roadsides.

The creature was a great spangled fritillary, one of many butterflies found in Southeast Minnesota. Others with similarly fanciful names are the tiger swallowtail, gray hairstreak, Aphrodite fritillary, pearl crescent, question mark, mourning cloak, painted lady, red admiral, tawny emperor, little wood satyr, wild indigo duskywing, clouded sulfur, and hackberry emperor.

Butterflies had begun to capture my attention the summer before, on days when birds were sparse. They gave me something besides birds to watch for, marvel at, and identify. My interest grew after I bought Jeffrey Glassberg's *Butterflies through Binoculars* (1999).

Just as bird enthusiasts once identified song birds by shooting them and preserving their skins, butterfly enthusiasts netted, chloroformed and pinned butterflies to display boards. *Butterflies through Binoculars* is the first major field guide to focus on netless

Great Spangled Fritillary

butterflying. Glassberg advocates the use of close-focusing binoculars that present a sharp image six feet away.

The book has an extensive introduction that includes such topics as butterfly finding; butterfly biology, life cycle, and behavior; and butterfly gardening, photography and conservation.

The butterfly life cycle includes the egg, caterpillar, pupa and adult stages. An adult female that has mated spends much time looking for the appropriate plant on which to lay her eggs. She recognizes the plant by sight and smell. The plant will provide food for the newly hatched caterpillars, which will hatch in less than a week and begin eating voraciously.

As a caterpillar eats and grows, its old skin splits and is shed several times. When it reaches full size, the caterpillar will attach itself to a twig or a blade of grass, where it will become encased in a hard outer shell (chrysalis) and become a pupa. At this stage, many changes occur over a period of a week or two, until the chrysalis splits open and an adult butterfly emerges.

Sometimes the pupa enters a resting stage for a few months or over a winter. Adult butterflies live anywhere from a few weeks to eight months. Some species have more than one brood per season.

Depending upon the species and other factors, the length of a butterfly's front wing varies from less that ½ inch to almost 3 inches. All butterflies have four wings and two antennas with clubs on the ends.

* * *

During a walk along our township road, I saw ahead of me a shimmering that looked like a classic mirage. The road seemed to be alive and, when I approached the spot, I discovered a large concentration of cabbage white butterflies fluttering their wings around a small puddle. When I carefully stepped around this little community, its members rose and flew all around me. I could feel their light touches and the little puffs of wind made by hundreds of small wings.

Farther down the road, I saw a similar concentration, this time of the much larger and more spectacular tiger swallowtails. According to Glassberg, butterflies often congregate at mud puddles—for the salt they get there, as well as the water.

* * *

Another common butterfly behavior is basking. Butterflies bask in the sun because they are cold-blooded and their body temperatures depend on the ambient temperatures. Some butterflies bask with their wings open. Others sit in the sun with their wings closed, tilting their bodies so that the plane of their wings is perpendicular to the sun.

Hill-topping is something else butterflies do. Glassberg wrote that, to the butterfly, hilltops are like singles bars, where the males patrol looking for females or sit and wait for the females to come to them. Unmated females also fly up to hilltops, while those already mated are busy looking for host plants and nectar.

Butterfly gardens are becoming increasingly popular. Many common garden flowers attract butterflies. Native wildflowers and small inconspicuous weeds are also good. The best gardens include caterpillar food plants. Unlike many moth caterpillars, most butterfly caterpillars will not destroy the plants they are eating.

The more complex a garden is, the more attractive it is to butterflies. Because butterflies fly from early spring to late fall, a garden should contain a procession of flowers that bloom through the seasons.

Glassberg says the purpose of his book is to make readers passionate about butterflies so that they will defend them. Many species have declined or have become extinct due habitat destruction, anti-mosquito spraying, pollution, large swaths of artificial lawns (biological desserts that support almost no butterflies) and immoral collectors. Often, the extinction of a single species will result in the removal of other species that are, in some way, dependent on the first.

Following Glassberg's introductory notes are his accounts of individual species, which include detailed descriptions, preferred habitat, range, abundance, and major food plants.

Following the species accounts are 71 plates of Glassberg's own photos. He has included several photos for each species, showing them with wings open, closed, from the top and from below. Accompanying the photos are short descriptions and distribution maps. This section is my favorite part of the book.

For me, butterfly watching is almost as compelling as bird watching. I have tried to approach butterfly watching on a more casual basis, but the temptation is there to delve deeply and to begin making lists.

Just as with birds, when I began putting names to butterflies, I was surprised at how many there are and how few I had noticed before.

Carol

I had just finished mowing the lawn on a hot and humid summer day. My hair was plastered to my head with sweat. I had taken off my sweaty clothes and was about to take a shower when there was a knock on the door. I threw my sweaty clothes back on.

My visitor was Carol Schumacher from Winona. I hadn't seen Carol since I first met her on a Minnesota Ornithologists' Union field trip seven years earlier. She said she had decided it was time to visit the Big Woods when she noticed that I had joined Winona's Hiawatha Valley Audubon Society.

Carol's friend and mentor Anne Marie Plunkett had also been telling her for years that she must come see our woods. We did not know it yet, but this day was the beginning of a friendship that would grow stronger each time we met.

In the few years before Carol's visit, my interest in birds had not been as strong as my interest in collecting bones. Carol was about to pull me back into birding with an irresistible force. She would teach me the difference between northern and Louisiana waterthrush calls; show me how and where look for nests; teach me to look in the sheltered dips of roads for winter birds; and sharpen my eye for hawks.

Although she likes birding with others, Carol is also a solo birder. Through careful patient hours of birding alone, she has learned what the field guides don't teach. She knows the soft communications of parent birds to their young. She knows to look for the relatively large red-tailed hawks perching on substantial branches and lighter rough-legged hawks perching on smaller branches in the tops of trees. She knows not only the hiccup call of the winter wren, but that the call is always accompanied by a little bounce.

Carol is devoted to every aspect of birding—identification through song and sight, habitat, behavior, nests, breeding patterns, flight patterns and migration. Carol is known in the Minnesota birding community for her work on the Department of Natural Resources breeding bird surveys, her Bluffland Bird Trips and the creation and management of "MnBird," the first Minnesota birding

Common Mergansers

network. She is also a recipient of the T. S. Roberts Award for lifetime contribution to Minnesota birding/ornithology.

In the days and weeks following her first visit, Carol and I often went birding together. Our most memorable experience occurred one November 14, when we met in Winona and decided to explore around Lake Pepin on the Mississippi River.

First, we walked along the dike that leads across the river to the dam at Alma, Wisconsin. The area was lively with passerines: red-bellied, downy and hairy woodpeckers, one yellow-shafted flicker, a belted kingfisher, blue jays, white-breasted nuthatches, cardinals, tree sparrows, juncos and goldfinch.

Looking out across the water, we spotted pied-billed grebes, tundra swans, mallards, canvasbacks, common goldeneyes and common mergansers. We counted 50 bald eagles in one place and hundreds of ring-billed gulls.

As the day progressed, the southeast wind increased. While watching the turbulent disorganized waves at Central Point, I thought about the times Art and I had had to fight the angry river while trying to maneuver our sailboat beyond the point into calmer water.

As Carol and I wandered up and down the lake, we began to notice an increasing number of common mergansers flying south against the wind. Mergansers are fish-eating diving ducks that usually fly fast and low over water in single file with their bodies held straight and horizontal. They have thin, hooked, red bills. The males have dark green heads and dark upper parts contrasting sharply with white, sometimes salmon-pink, flanks and breast. Females are gray and white with a crested chestnut head and chestnut neck.

We stopped and got out of the car to watch. The wind was like a slap in the face. Carol called out, "They're streaming by like pulled taffy. The more you pull, the more you see!"

I timed her for 10 seconds while she tried to count. "I got about 150," she said, "but I only counted one line and I think there are many lines all across the lake."

That meant at least 900 ducks a minute and they kept coming. The scene imprinted itself on our brains: thousands of wings beating, thousands of necks stretched into the wind; color, sound, movement—all our senses alert and intermixed; gulls mingled with the ducks, looking like pieces of confetti; bald eagles weaving in and out.

The ducks dropped to the water, then rose as a single entity, a field of white, chestnut, salmon-pink and black, vibrating low over the lake as far as our eyes could see.

Were we part of it, part of the scene? We watched without talking as the ducks dropped, rose, streamed by and dropped down again.

We peered into the lake. It was getting hard to see. We rubbed our eyes, then looked at our watches and realized we had lost our sense of time. It was 5 o'clock, almost dark.

On our drive back home, it began to snow—the first snow of the season.

Big Woods Celebrities

On a morning walk on June 2, 1989, I stopped to rest on a bench deep in my woods. The day was partly cloudy and breezy, with temperatures in the high 70s. The only sounds I heard came from birds, chipmunks, insects and the wind. I must have been hearing a particular song for a few moments before I consciously realized I was hearing something different. It was a long and clear "dee-da, dee-da, dee-dee-oh," with the second to last syllable higher and louder than the others.

I walked in the direction of a wooded ravine, looked up about 15 feet into the branches of a white oak and saw a singing male hooded warbler. Its bright yellow under parts and distinctive black hood enclosing a yellow face and forehead made for an easy identification.

I hurried home to call my friend and mentor, Anne Marie, who agreed with my identification of the first hooded warbler ever reported in Fillmore County. In a telephone call the same day, I spoke with University of Minnesota Ornithologist Bruce Fall, who has a special interest in this species.

Although the hooded warbler's normal range is south and east of Minnesota, it regularly wanders into the state. Bruce has regularly observed breeding pairs in the Minneapolis area. He said I should continue watching for the bird; since it was already June, we could have a nesting pair.

When Anne Marie came to look for the bird early the next day, she heard it, but was unable to find it. I never saw it again either, but I still think about it whenever I walk through the wooded ravine.

* * *

In the winter of 1989-1990, we didn't have much snow. All winter, it was easy to walk our woodland trails. On January 2, on

*Hooded Warbler and
False Solomon's-Seal*

the western edge of our property, I heard whistling calls I didn't recognize. I spotted a flock of birds in a grove of red cedars. At first, I thought they might be cedar waxwings, but the calls didn't fit. I looked more carefully and saw that the birds had gray plumage with yellowish heads and napes. They were larger and plumper than cedar waxwings and had short dark bills.

I consulted my field guides and discovered the birds were pine grosbeaks. I knew it was an unusual sighting, that pine grosbeaks only sporadically come this far south, but there they were, gorging on cedar berries. They stayed for about six weeks. Among the visitors who saw them were Anne Marie; her friend Ray Glassel,

Yellow-breasted Chat and Solomon's-Seal

who has seen more bird species in Minnesota than anyone else; Bob Janssen, longtime president of the Minnesota Ornithologists' Union (MOU); and our good friends, John and Chris Hockema.

* * *

One day in May almost a decade later, we watched a line of cars drive up our driveway. Thirty people, including their leader Kim Eckert, from Duluth, climbed out and walked towards our house. They were on an MOU field trip and had come here to see tufted titmice. Their base for the weekend was Forestville State Park.

Tufted titmice, members of the *Paridae f*amily, which also includes chickadees, are small birds somewhat larger than chickadees, but with similar behavior. They come to the feeders, grab a single seed and fly to a nearby branch where they open the seed with their bills while holding it with their feet. They are dark gray above, pale gray below, with buff-colored flanks, dark gray crests and big dark eyes. Their song is a loud whistled "peter-peter-peter" and they have numerous whistling and raspy calls.

Titmice are common in eastern and southern parts of North America. Although one had appeared at our feeders almost every winter, we didn't record a breeding pair until 1995. Since then, we have had a resident flock and they have spread throughout the Big Woods. Because titmice are casual or absent from other parts of Minnesota, many people have come here just to see these birds. The titmice, of course, know nothing of their fame and the friendships they generate.

I warned the group that the titmice are shy. They are accustomed to our sounds and actions and approach us closely, but when strangers are here, they are slow to appear.

While waiting, we visited with people we knew and some we met for the first time. Suddenly, we heard the song we had been waiting to hear, but it didn't sound quite right. Then we realized it was coming from Kim's tape recorder.

A moment later, from deep in the woods, we heard an answering bird. Male titmice are strongly territorial; I imagined the answering bird was on his way to chase the interloper out of his territory. Soon he appeared on the edge of our yard.

* * *

On May 22 of the same year, 24 members of the Minnesota River Valley Audubon Club (MRVAC) arrived at our house so quietly that we didn't see them until they were standing in our yard watching a titmouse eating sunflower seeds. Although they had found their target bird right away, the group took time to look for other birds.

They found a rose-breasted grosbeak and a redstart sitting on nests and watched the yellow-bellied sapsuckers fly in and out of their nest hole in a nearby poplar tree. Someone heard a buzzy two-part song and drew our attention to a singing blue-winged warbler, another specialty of Southeast Minnesota.

Our guests also took time to admire violets, May apples and trillium in bloom; Jack-in-the-pulpits just beginning to unfold; the maidenhair ferns that line our driveway; and the towering oaks of the Big Woods.

* * *

On June 5, Carol Schumacher brought one of her Blufflands Bird Trips to our house. Eight people sat on our porch listening for a tufted titmouse. It was a cool breezy space on a hot humid day, shaded by ironwood trees and tall oaks. The sun shot tiny rays through spaces not shaded by leaves. The porch is long and narrow, six feet above the ground, looking into deep woods.

A redstart came to the birdbath nestled among the trees. She was yellow and gray, small and delicate. Her mate, a splashy red and black, made his way through the woods to join her. He had taken this route before. Someone asked if we have deer and grouse here. I said yes, realizing that I take both species for granted.

Finally, we heard a faint titmouse song in the distance, so faint we weren't sure we had heard it at all. Then we heard it again and saw it making its way through the woods.

With some reluctance, we left the comfort of the porch to check on the rose-breasted grosbeak nest that the MRVAC group had found a couple weeks before. On the way, we stopped to listen to the sapsucker young crying for food from inside their nest hole. We watched the bluebirds carrying food to their nestlings in the bluebird house and a hummingbird sitting in its favorite place on the power line. The female grosbeak was on her nest, head up, watching us. I told my visitors that the male also takes his turn incubating. Sometimes he sings on his nest.

Two catbirds flew back and forth in front of us, chattering as catbirds do. They probably also had a nest nearby. When the group left, it took a while for me to see my yard through my own eyes again.

* * *

From mid-June through July, the titmice are quiet and secretive. The young are just leaving their nests and are more vulnerable than at any other time in their lives. In late summer, the birds become more visible and vocal again and the loud begging voices of the juveniles and calls of their parents can be heard throughout the woods. The family groups stay in loose flocks with other family groups through the winter. During this time, they frequent the feeders more often and treat our guests to close-up views as they line up to eat the peanut butter on our windowsills.

* * *

Our next notable bird arrived in mid-June 2000. During my morning walks, I began to hear a loud whistling sound coming from a brushy hillside near Blagsvedt Run, about a mile from my house.

The sound tapped into a vague memory that I could not place. For a while, I wondered if it was a frog. Then one day, while playing a recording of warbler songs, I heard the yellow-breasted chat and thought it could be my mystery bird. However, I only heard its whistles, not the typical squeaks, chatters and rattles.

Yellow-breasted chats are common in other parts of the country, but they are solitary, shy and hard to find. They are uncommon in Minnesota, where a sighting draws birders from all parts of the state.

On June 25, St. Cloud resident, Phil Chu, came to our woods to see the titmice. He had just been to see the chat reported in Great River Bluffs State Park overlooking the Mississippi near Winona.

I told Phil that it would be difficult to see the titmice, as they were in their reclusive and secretive phase. He said he was a patient person; he was willing to wait as long as it took. While we waited, I told him about my mystery bird. He agreed that it might be a chat and offered to help me identify it.

After almost an hour, the titmice began coming to the feeders. When Phil had seen enough, we drove to the brushy hill near Blagsvedt Run to look for the mystery bird. Phil played a recording of a chat. Before long, we heard a whistled response and the bird came within sight. We watched it for about half an hour. At its closest, it was about 20 feet away. We had good views and were able to hear its full repertoire of sounds. We could see its long tail and thick bill, olive upper parts and white cheek stripes bordering a bright yellow throat. It became obvious why the field guides say this bird is our largest warbler.

One can never plan for backyard rarities. When you see one, you must call the birders and they will come. Our friends, John and Chuck from Rochester, were the first visitors to see the chat. Over the next 12 days, at least 22 people saw the bird. Some called before they came. Others I found on my walks along the township road.

On July 6, Carol Schumacher and I heard the chat in its usual place on the brushy hill. For a while, we thought we heard two of them, but we couldn't say for sure. This was the last time anyone was able to locate the bird.

* * *

Autumn came and went without any noteworthy sightings. Winter arrived. On December 29, I looked out my bedroom window and saw a flock of cedar waxwings in our crab apple tree. Carol had repeatedly told me to look closely at flocks of cedar waxwings because Bohemian waxwings could be among them. The Bohemians are northwestern birds that occasionally wander into our area in winter. I have always diligently looked for them, but without any luck.

Not expecting to see anything unusual, I dutifully looked through my binoculars and saw, not one, but six Bohemians, a life bird for me. Their large size, gray under parts and cinnamon undertail coverts made them easy to identify. They stayed three days, stripping the tree of all its remaining apples.

* * *

Since then, I've been waiting for my next backyard rarity. A loggerhead shrike or a varied thrush would be nice. Maybe a hooded warbler will appear in the wooded ravine. But, I feel in my heart that it will be the yellow-breasted chat returning to the brushy hill with his whistles, chucks, squeaks and squawks.

Big Woods Characters

Soon after we bought our land, I realized that the human inhabitants of the Big Woods were almost as much a part of it as the animals and plants. I usually found old Rueben, the first neighbor I met, sitting just outside his open door watching wasps and swallows freely flying in and out of his house.

Bobby Norby, the second neighbor I met was, and still is, a historian of the Big Woods. He lives with his wife Phyllis on a hill above Wisel Creek. Their children, grandchildren and great grandchildren live nearby.

Bobby has told me many stories about the woods. From him, I have learned about timber rattlers, ginseng, Indian artifacts, the occasional bear and moonshine stills.

When Rueben was alive, Bobby dropped by to check on him almost every day. One day I brought my friend and new neighbor, Kathy Erickson, to meet Rueben. While we were visiting, Bobby arrived with a sack of potatoes dug from his patch down by the Wisel. From then on, Kathy referred to him as the "Potato Man."

In spite of its outlaw reputation, the Big Woods posed little danger by the time we arrived. However, from time to time, it still housed eccentrics. One was Charlie, a burned-out Wall Street businessman, who returned to the woods of his birth to live in a teepee in what used to be Clara Vickerman's yard.

After the teepee, Charlie lived in a two-story dwelling he built out of his car. He had lost his driver's license, so his only means of transportation was a bicycle, which he rode all over the county. He politely told me once, he didn't think we could be friends if I wasn't willing to get drunk with him. One day, when he found me sitting by the stream, he said, "You look like the essence of serenity."

Charlie's sister Betty used to live off and on in Clara's old house. She hung frilly curtains in the windows, planted a garden near the old barn, raised chickens and placed ornaments in the yard.

Before Charlie and Betty, Melvin Thorson, an old Norwegian bachelor farmer, lived in a dilapidated mobile home next to Clara's old barn. I usually found him sitting in a lawn chair just outside his door. Everyone who passed on the township road stopped to visit with Melvin. He had a black cocker spaniel that was old and fat, just like his master. The poor dog always had multiple woodticks growing thick and swollen on his blood.

Clara's Barn

Melvin's cousin, Sven, used to go fishing with Rueben's son, Pancake, on the Mississippi River. One day, while they were fishing and drinking, Pancake turned around in the boat to talk with Sven, who had suddenly vanished. His body was dragged out of the river the next day.

Alton and Rosie Housker used to live on a farm about two miles from us, as the crow flies. They were soon to retire and move to town. One day, we received a call from Rosie asking if we had lost a cat. She said there was a Siamese cat in their field who looked sick.

Art jumped into the car and sped over to Housker's where he found Izzy, our beloved 19-year-old cat, who had slipped out of the door nine days earlier when no one was looking. We had searched for him long and hard, but his old ears probably couldn't hear us calling and his old eyes couldn't show him the way home. It remains a mystery how he survived nine days on his own and how he managed to escape the talons of great horned owls.

Jaymour Larson, another old Norwegian bachelor farmer, lived at the end of the minimum maintenance road, just past Bratrud's. He used to make daily rounds in his old car, driving down the road just so far, then driving back. He waved only when waved to. His shy eyes looked away.

Jaymour and his brother, also a bachelor, farmed together for many years on the place where they were born. When his brother died, Jaymour stayed on alone. I wondered what he did over there all day and all night. He was too old to farm anymore. Did he walk to the creek and listen to it as I do? Did he hear the coyotes call? He knew about the heronry nearby. What else did he know? Not long after he went to live in a nursing home, Jaymour passed away.

Ted Thompson, also a Norwegian bachelor farmer, lived alone in his house at the end of a road not far from Norby's. Every day he got into his truck and drove through the Big Woods, leaving some hay for a horse or caring for someone's dog. He had a little dog of his own.

Ted stopped to talk with everyone he met, until he got Lou Gehrig's disease and could no longer talk. After that, he drove his truck without stopping or waving, until one day he could no longer drive. A niece and her family came to take care of him— the man who had always taken care of others. When the doctor said he had to leave his little house for a nursing home, Ted went out to the barn and took his own life.

Martin Ackerman and his sons also patrolled the Big Woods road. They picked up odd jobs mowing lawns, trimming trees and fixing fences. They often passed me in their old pickup when I was out walking. Sometimes I would climb partway up a bluff and sit on a log, perfectly visible from the road, if anyone thought to look. Martin and his boys were the only ones who ever noticed me there.

Martin and Brenda have five children, four boys and one girl. They used to live in a mobile home down by the bridge, across from Rueben's old place. One evening, Art and I were walking down the road when we heard a pickup truck speeding toward us, scattering gravel and raising dust. It passed us, rounded a bend, and crashed into Brenda and her children in their rusty red Ford.

When we reached the scene, Martin was already there and the pickup driver was yelling at Brenda: "It's your fault! You were driving on the wrong side of the road!"

I quickly looked around thinking I would have to administer first aid or call an ambulance, but I saw no blood, no broken bones, and no one lying in the ditch.

"You were going too fast," Art said to the driver. "I'm going to call the sheriff and report the accident." With a look of surprise, the driver backed away. We returned home and called the sheriff who came out and took our statements.

The next day, I came across the boys fishing with sticks and strings on Rueben's former property. I sat on a rock while they fished and talked: "Our dad said we have a right to fish here. That guy who owns this land says he can keep us off, but our dad says he can't. Once our dad saw a bunch of girls bare-naked up there in that big round tub they built. There's lots a fish here in the crick. We catch 'em and our mom cooks 'em. We know where you live. You live up there on the hill."

Soon after this visit, the Ackermans moved into another mobile home at the other end of the Big Woods road. There they put up a shiny red mailbox with large black letters, "USOB," printed on its side. A fence crossed their driveway. A sign on the fence read "Beware of Vicious Dog."

Not long after the Ackermans moved, several families of the Moger clan got together and bought the land where the Ackermans had lived. Although the Mogers were newcomers to the Big Woods, it seemed as though they had been here forever.

They used the land mostly for recreation. No one lived there year around until Rockny Moger, with the help of friends, built a large house with a deck overlooking the South Fork. Rockny has a reputation for being kind to animals. Sometimes people abandon unwanted pets near the Moger property because they know Rockny cannot let an animal go hungry.

When they come for weekends or a week here and there, the Mogers stay in a variety of vans, trailers and campers. They hunt, fish, build huge campfires and tear up and down the road in ATVs. They are always in the process of making improvements and cleaning up their part of the woods, which they have littered with broken chairs, old refrigerators, children's toys, beer cans and junk cars. Before they have finished these tasks, they are usually cheerfully on to other projects.

Minneapolis weekenders, Kim Kluender and his extended family, bought Rueben's old place. They mowed the lawn, planted trees and daffodils, built a hot tub and a sauna, put an addition on the house, installed a big red gate and decorated everything with antlers and skulls.

Opossum

One winter day on my morning walk, I found a dead opossum near the red gate. It looked as though it was only asleep, but I saw blood merging with snow under its pink nose. I carried it to the side of the road so tires wouldn't open it up and spill its guts. Then I looked up and saw furniture and skulls spilled on Kluender's lawn. Windows were broken. The door was wide open. Across the road at Moger's, I also saw furniture on the lawn, open doors and broken windows. I returned home and called the sheriff, but the perpetrators were never apprehended.

One Sunday, I heard rock music blaring through the woods. I assumed it was coming from Moger's, but when I went to investigate, I found six Amish teenagers, three boys and three girls dressed in Sunday clothes, standing by their buggies listening to a boombox and drinking beer.

When I saw them throwing beer cans into the woods, I scolded, "Pick those beer cans up! You know better than that!"

They looked surprised and immediately did as I asked.

Sometimes, I meet my neighbor, Marnelle Mcneilus, jogging down the road. He and his family built a big house where Rosheims used to live and named their place Mercy Valley Farm.

One day, Marnelle stopped long enough to say, "I enjoyed your article about habitat for trout and birds. You know, we depend on you to take care of the woods."

Amish Neighbors

On an unseasonably warm September day, I was sitting in my office/sunroom half-clothed, writing at my computer, when I head knocking on the kitchen door. Then I heard Art's voice saying, "Do you want to talk with her?"

I quickly grabbed a pair of shorts and went to the kitchen, where I found a man with a long beard dressed in black holding his flat top straw hat in his hands. I invited him to sit with me at my kitchen table.

It suddenly dawned on me that my visitor was here in response to an article I had written for the *Fillmore County Journal* in which I mentioned the Amish kids who were drinking beer along the Big Woods road.

My visitor wanted to know more about this incident so he could determine if some of his kids were involved. I asked how many children he had.

He said, "Fourteen."

When I gave him more details, he seemed satisfied that the culprits were not his children. I assured him that the teenagers had been polite and that I hadn't been angry, only surprised.

My guest told me a little about "runsprungen," or "running around," a period of time from about age 14 to the early 20s, when Amish young people have extra freedom to experience the outside world. They may learn to drive a car, for example, or take a job working for the English (what the Amish call the rest of us). They may go to movies or engage in other "English" types of entertainment.

Runsprungen is also a courting or dating time, during which young people have "singings" in the various homes. The boys and girls may pair up for these gatherings and this pairing may eventually lead to marriage.

The Amish believe the period of freedom will allow their young people to make informed decisions and firm commitments to the Amish way of life when it comes time for them to be baptized and join the community as adults. Even with this freedom, my visitor said, the kids are not supposed to be drinking beer.

"I didn't want to get anybody in trouble," I said. "That was not my intention." He replied that the kids would be held accountable, but would not be in serious trouble.

In 1974, because of over-population in their Wayne County, Ohio communities, Amish families began moving to Fillmore County. What drew them here were the wooded areas for lumber and fuel, springs for animals and refrigeration, small farms, good soil and reasonable land prices. The families that moved here are of the Old Order, which is the most conservative.

The Mennonites and Amish have their roots in the Anabaptist faith, which dates back to the 15th century in Europe. The Anabaptists believed in adult baptism. Followers were baptized only when they were old enough to make a conscious commitment to Christ and enter the body of believers, where there was mutual care, exhortation and accountability. For Anabaptists, the Christian life was a new birth leading to a new life of discipleship. Because of their beliefs, they were persecuted as heretics by the Catholic Church.

In 1525, during the Protestant Reformation in Zurich, Switzerland, Menno Simmons, a former Dutch Catholic priest, broke away from a radical group of Anabaptists and founded the Mennonites. In 1693, the Amish broke away from the Mennonites. Their founder was Jacob Amman, a Swiss

Mennonite bishop. Today, the foundations of Mennonite and Amish faiths remain the same as that of the early Anabaptists.

What primarily separates the Amish from other people is their belief in living in the world, but not being *of* the world. They believe certain Bible passages call them to a life of separation and denial. For example, in I John 2:15-17, it says,

> Do not love the world or the things in the world. If anyone loves the world, love for the Father is not in him. For all that is in the world, the lust of the flesh and the lust of the eyes and the pride of life, is not of the Father, but is of the world. And the world passes away, and the lust of it; but he who does the will of God abides forever.

The Old Order Amish have what they call the "Ordnung," which are unwritten rules and regulations determined by the church elders regarding what may or may not be threats to their way of life. Often there are fine lines between what one may or may not do. For example, it is okay to ride in a car for temporary necessities having to do with work, health, funerals, weddings and other serious matters, but to accept a ride for pleasure is too convenient or frivolous and is therefore unnecessary. Generally, an Amish person may take one step into the modern world, but not 10 steps, and he/she must always remember to come back to the life of separation and self-denial.

One way the Amish remain separate from the world at large is by speaking German in their homes. Youngsters learn English only when they start going to school. The Amish have their own one-room schoolhouses and their teachers have no formal training. Children learn the basic skills of reading, writing and arithmetic. Formal education ends after 8th grade.

Amish Horse and Buggy

The life of separation does not mean the Amish are separate from each other. Indeed, sameness in their clothing, home furnishings and livelihood is required, to take away the lures of worldly ways concerning fashion, material goods, modern conveniences and entertainment. They strive to maintain a cohesive community and discourage the singling out of any one person. For this reason, I have not used any personal names here.

Dress styles, consisting of dark colors, are identical within the group. Women and girls wear long dark-colored dresses. Instead of buttons, they fasten their clothes with hook and eye closures, straight pins and safety pins. Women may also wear capes. Women and girls wear prayer kapps and, when away from home, wide-brimmed black bonnets.

Neither women nor men have collars or lapels. All shoes are black and children often go barefoot from spring into fall. Little boys wear dresses until they are toilet-trained. Men use hooks and eyes to fasten their dark coats, jackets, shirts and trousers. Their undergarments have buttons. Men and boys wear flat top homemade straw hats in summer and black felt hats in cold weather.

Amish homes within a group look the same inside and out. They commonly consist of five bedrooms with closets, a large main room, a large kitchen, a pantry and an open porch that extends across the front of the house. The paned windows are Amish-made and lumber is home-sawn or purchased pine. The houses contain Amish-made furniture, navy blue curtains and have bare oak floors. They have no central heating or electricity. They use woodburning stoves for cooking and heating.

The Amish use horses to farm and for local travel. They hold church in their homes and have their own cemeteries. The only national newspaper they read is *The Budget*, a weekly paper that publishes Amish-Mennonite news across the country. They may also read local newspapers, such as the *Fillmore County Journal*.

Amish people do many things collectively, such as quilting, cooking and harvesting. Their get-togethers for the construction of buildings are called "frolics" because they are also social occasions. While the men build, the women quilt, cook and serve food.

According to Amish beliefs, if a person decides to leave the community, he is shunned because he has fallen from God's favor. The basis for the practice of shunning, or "meidung" comes from I Corinthians 5:11:

> But rather I wrote to you not to associate with anyone who bears the name of brother if he is guilty of immorality or greed, or is an idolater, reviler, drunkard, or robber—not even to eat with such a one.

Meidung is especially strict for a person who has already been baptized. He cannot eat or drink with other baptized adults. During a visit, he must sit at a separate table, usually at a table with the children. No one may take anything directly from his hand. He cannot conduct business with another Amish person. Although he may return for a visit or a funeral, he will make his family more comfortable if he dresses in Amish-style clothes. In spite of these strict rules, forgiveness is quick for those who repent.

As the Amish father and I visited at our kitchen table, Art entered the conversation with questions about *The Martyrs' Mirror*, a book, published in Dutch in 1660 by Thielman J. van Braght. The book contains more than 1,100 pages describing the persecutions and torture of early Christians and Anabaptists.

Our guest was quick to respond to Art's questions and seemed pleased with our interest. He said the book is familiar to all Amish people and is present in most homes. He said they read it in German, but an English translation is available.

I expressed my admiration for people who can speak and read two languages. I know from experience as a German teacher how difficult it is to teach and learn a foreign language. Our visitor and I tried to speak some German with each other and quickly found our dialects so different that we could understand very little. Our guest said he could not understand visitors from Germany, but he could read German even better than English.

When he stood up to leave, our visitor asked if it would be all right for his wife and him to come see us some Sunday. We said we would like that.

As I watched him drive away in his horse-drawn buggy, I had to resist the impulse to grab my camera and take a picture. The second of the Ten Commandments, Deuteronomy 5:8, reads:

You shall not make for yourself a graven image, or any likeness of anything that is in heaven above, or that is on the earth beneath, or that is in the water under the earth.

For this reason, Amish people do not want their pictures taken; they put no faces on dolls; they do not have mirrors, except for shaving; and they do not own cameras. Photos of Amish farms, buggies and horses do appear in books and on postcards. And children often draw pictures of their farms and animals, but no likenesses of any people.

The Amish view the intrusion of tourism into their lives with mixed feelings. They accept that tourism gives them a market for their crafts and a means for paying bills when times are hard. They do not generally advertise their own crafts, but agree to let local stores market crafts for them. They allow people into their homes to purchase crafts and baked goods, but do not encourage people to come if they aren't interested in buying something.

A couple weeks after the Amish father's visit, I heard someone knocking on my kitchen door and looked out to find a man with a long beard dressed in black holding his straw hat in his hands. It didn't take me long to realize why he was here. He too was concerned that some of his children were among the beer drinking teenagers. Of his 13 children, twin girls and three boys are in their teens. I said I appreciated his concern and offered him the same assurances I did my first visitor.

We talked a little about the pleasures of country life. When he admired our home, we talked about the rewards of building our own houses. I invited him to come again.

In the course of these two visits, I saw two fathers who demanded responsible behavior and accountability from their children and for whom it was important to coexist harmoniously with the wider community.

Amish children begin to play responsible roles in their families at an early age. Their confidence in these roles is apparent. Once, Art and I came upon an Amish boy who looked about 10 years old. His horse-drawn wagon had sunk into the soft springtime shoulder of a county road. When we stopped to help, the boy directed Art to watch his horses. I can still picture Art standing there trying to act nonchalant while looking up at the two huge draft horses whose reins he held.

The youngster then directed me to drive to the next farm and ask the farmer to come with his tractor to pull the wagon out of the mud. The boy thus calmly orchestrated his own rescue with no apparent anxiety.

I have never passed an Amish person who didn't wave to me. Whenever I meet with an Amish buggy while walking down the Big Woods road, its occupants always greet me, often by name. Today, in rural Canton and Harmony, common sights include Amish children carrying books and lunch boxes as they walk barefoot to school; women hanging clothes to dry on the long porches that extend across the fronts of their homes; or farmers cultivating with draft horses in distant fields like pictures from yesteryear.

Crossing Cultures

It was a cold and wet October evening in 1979. Members of the Sheie and Garness Lutheran churches of rural Mabel waited in the LaCrosse, Wisconsin, airport for a family coming across Laotian mountains, the Mekong River, and centuries of cultural territory, to live in the land of opportunity. The two churches were making it possible for a Hmong family to leave their refugee camp in Laos.

Suddenly, there they were—a husband, wife, daughter and grandmother—four real people, not just names on pieces of paper. The Minnesotans looked gigantic as they hovered over the little Hmong family.

The Hmong are an ancient people who migrated out of South-central Eurasia into western China thousands of years ago. In China, they were treated sometimes with hospitality, at other times with hostility. During the 19th century, some migrated into Laos, where they were able to live in peace because they farmed in the high elevations that other Laotian people generally did not use.

When the French colonized Southeast Asia, the Hmong resisted. They resisted again when the Japanese occupied Laos in the 1940s and when the French returned after World War II.

Throughout these struggles, the Hmong people determinedly held on to their cultural identity.

In the 1960s, the U.S. government recruited Hmong men to rescue American pilots shot down on bombing missions over North Vietnam. Approximately 100 Hmong died for every American pilot they saved.

When the United States withdrew from the Vietnam War in 1975, it also withdrew support for its Hmong allies, leaving them open to persecution by the Communists. Many Hmong retreated to the jungles, where they hid and fought as guerrillas.

Many looked for refuge in neutral Thailand, but to get there they had to cross the Mekong River, which is about the same size as the Mississippi. They attempted to cross the river in boats and rafts made from bamboo stalks and plastic bags. Some tried to swim across. About 50,000 people made it to Thailand. About 50,000 died trying.

Chou Vang, his wife Xia, their 11-year-old daughter Ahzoua and Grandmother Mia were among the lucky ones who made it safely into Laos, but not without the loss of two sons.

As we stood in the LaCrosse airport trying to communicate with each other in spite of our language barrier, we could see our guests were tired and somewhat bewildered. It was time for Pastor Jay to drive them back to Mabel and the house we had prepared for them.

We had spent many hours preparing for this family's arrival. We had cleaned, painted and decorated the house we rented for them. The house contained furniture, bedding, kitchen utensils and dishes donated by members of the congregations. The cupboards and refrigerator contained food that we hoped they would understand how to use. We had found a janitor's job for Chou in a nearby town.

In spite of our preparations, doubts crept in. Would this family feel welcome in our small southeastern Minnesota community that rarely saw anyone who wasn't Caucasian? What would the good Christians in this community think of the Hmong religion, called animism, based on the belief that natural phenomena and objects such as rocks, trees, and the wind are alive and have spirits?

Could we step outside ourselves enough to understand this family's needs? Their experience of the world was very different from ours. They were not accustomed to running water, flush toilets, or electricity. They did not know how to drive cars and had never been to a movie. They knew firsthand about war and hiding from the enemy.

After providing food, shelter and clothing, our most important task was to teach our guests English. It was my job to coordinate their language teaching program. In preparation, I had studied techniques for teaching English as a second language. I had also learned something about the Hmong language, a tonal language in which any small error of enunciation may completely change a meaning. This would become obvious to me when my efforts to learn Hmong phrases sent my students into fits of laughter.

In lieu of a written language, which the Hmong did not have until the 1950s, their custom was to pass their history on through story telling and through the intricate patterns of the Pandau, or brightly colored fibers woven into ceremonial cloth.

A few days after our trip to LaCrosse, I timidly knocked on the Vang's kitchen door. I had prepared lesson plans in detail, knowing other volunteers would use them also. Not only would I teach the Vangs English; I would also have to teach the volunteers how to teach.

In spite of my immense size compared to Xia, and her dependency on me, she answered the door with more dignity than I could summon for myself. Ahzoua stood behind Xia and I could see Grandmother Mia in the next room sitting in a rocking chair, working on her Pandau. Chou was already working at his new job. I would have little opportunity to teach him, but he would learn from his co-workers and his wife and daughter.

Pointing to my books and myself, I said, "My name is Nancy. I will teach you English."

Xia and Ahzoua nodded their heads and offered me a seat at their kitchen table. Mia nodded to me from the living room. I would soon realize she had no intention of learning English. I would not press her.

My students were enthusiastic and quickly learned the cardinal numbers, how to use our money, how to tell time, the days of the week, the seasons, our customary greetings, and the many ways Minnesotans talk about the weather. But, they had difficulty constructing sentences.

One day I had an idea. I bought two hand puppets, which would make it easier for me to demonstrate dialogues. The puppets were successful. Ahzoua began to invent her own dialogues, using a puppet in each hand. She and her mother were proud of their progress.

In spite of past tragedies and new challenges, my students presented indomitable spirits and a surprising playfulness. One day as we sat at the kitchen table, Ahzoua and Xia began talking together in their own language. They looked at me and giggled.

Xia left the room and returned with a bundle of clothes. Before long, they had dressed me in the brilliantly colored materials of a Hmong ceremonial costume. A glance in the mirror told me how incongruous I looked—a large blond American wearing the clothes of the small, delicate, dark-skinned Hmong. We laughed and snapped a picture. I considered this occasion an honor.

As time moved on, we tried to find the right balance between teaching and providing the Vangs with rest and privacy. We also offered them some fun times with potluck dinners and other social occasions.

When another refugee family moved into nearby Spring Grove, the Vangs had an opportunity to socialize in their own language. The two families became fast friends. I think this friendship helped to dispel some of their loneliness.

We had recently heard that a number of Hmong men had mysteriously died in this country. No one could find a cause for their deaths, other than homesickness.

I could understand their reason for homesickness. The culture they left is very different from ours. In their culture, social life is based on the extended family or clan. All the people in a clan are considered immediate relatives.

The usual home contains members of several nuclear families and several generations, all contributing to the support of the extended family. Both men and women hold important positions in their villages. They are gardeners, blacksmiths, jewelers, wood-workers, weavers of the Pandau and sewers of daily garments and ceremonial clothing. The men are all skilled hunters and trappers.

Spirits inhabit all areas of the Hmong world. Because human illness is the result of bad spirits, there is little division between medicine and religion. Some of the people are herbal doctors and shamans who have special access to the spirit world and know how to call up good spirits and drive away bad ones.

Village life is highly ceremonial and has precise rules. For example, at a funeral, a qeej (a musical instrument) player first plays the "Life Stops" song. The second song is "Thanks to the Spirits of the House," in which thanks is given to the spirits of the beds, the fireplaces, the centerpost, the altar and the main door. The third song tells the dead person's spirit to go and get the placenta from the birthplace. In the last song, the qeej player helps the dead person get to the ancestors' place.

I thought about how removed we are from the natural world compared to the Hmong. We read a book or watch a movie. They tell stories. We buy our tools and clothes from stores. They make their own tools and clothes. We buy our meat from the grocery store. They hunt for their meat. For music, we listen to CD players or radios. If they want music, they make their own. We go to church for spirituality and to doctors for the care of our bodies. For them the mind and body are one.

Over time, the Vangs became more Americanized, at least on the surface. Ahzoua was doing well in school. Some racial slurs had been directed at her, but she had a group of friends who were supportive and came to her defense. Chou continued to work hard and reliably at his job. When spring came, Xia planted a garden. We had a picnic. We made plans for the future.

Then one day, we learned that the Vangs were moving to St. Paul, where they had relatives. Grandmother Mia had the power to say they must go. They would thus become part of an internal migration as separated families sought to regroup within this country. The Hmong people were still trying to maintain their cultural identity, just as they had throughout their long and difficult history.

Before they left, the Vangs and their friends in Spring Grove planned a feast for us. They bought food at a Southeast Asian grocery in LaCrosse, then spent days preparing it. When the feast day arrived, the good people of Scheie and Garness Lutheran Churches crowded into the Vang's backyard. Two long tables held mountains of food. We ate food we had never eaten before. The mountains disappeared.

I looked at our diverse group and thought we weren't so different from each other after all. The same camaraderie present in a village in Laos could be present in the little town of Mabel.

We had done a good deed in sponsoring the Vangs, but they had given to us as well. They had stretched our boundaries and brought us out of ourselves. We had all changed since we first met on that cold October evening in the LaCrosse airport.

Saying good-by was hard for me. I shook Chou's hand and hugged Ahzoua and Mia. By the time I reached Xia, we were both crying. That day was the last time we would see each other. Xia quietly told me that she didn't want to leave.

PastureLand

Lush grassland pastures cover the rolling hills of Springside Farm on the southern edge of the Big Woods. Fences divide large fields into smaller paddocks. Lanes (larger than paths, smaller than roads) provide access to the fields.

Springside Farm, named for its numerous springs, has been home to Bonnie and Vance Haugen and their three children since 1993. The 230-acre farm is part of PastureLand, a co-op of four farms and six families founded in 1999. The co-op's mission is to provide consumers with quality dairy products from local family farms while providing cows with comfortable low-stress lives, the land with good stewardship and the farmers with income and good working conditions.

On a warm day in early November, the word "balance" came to my mind as I looked across the hills at 50 cows methodically grazing in one of the paddocks. Sun and shadow swept across the green hills while I waited for Bonnie, the main farmer in the family, who soon drove up on her four-wheeler to give me a tour of the farm. She briefly described their sustainable farming methods.

"We intensively manage and graze our dairy animals," she said. "That means we plant grasses and legumes such as clover and alfalfa for the cows to eat. We fence so the cows get only a small area at a time. This allows the plants to regrow during their rest time. This differs from the old pastures where the grasses are often lacking in rest periods, which depletes their root reserves, curtailing available feed stores in the pastures."

The Haugens grow all their own legumes and grasses, except for a small amount of corn. The varying soils on the farm determine which crops they plant and where they are planted. The grass crops include reed canarygrass, orchardgrass, bromes, ryes and timothy. Some grasses, such as reed canarygrass, which has very deep roots, can grow on their own for many years. Alfalfa and clovers (legumes) periodically need a boost of additional seeds. Certain crops, such as alfalfa and orchardgrass, are planted together. This diversity of plants contrasts with the row crop monocultures found on feedlot dairies.

I climbed onto the four-wheeler behind Bonnie and we drove down one of the lanes to feed 31 calves that were grazing in a nearby paddock. Pep, a young Border Collie, accompanied us. When we reached the paddock, Bonnie opened a bag of mixed grains and trace minerals. She said she would supplement the calves' diet of grasses and hay two times a day in this way until they came close to "freshening."

Bonnie called, "Little boss, come on, come on, come on," in a rhythm-like a song and the calves gathered to eat.

Bonnie breeds the calves at about one year of age, at which time they will be called "heifers." Gestation is nine months. A heifer

Holstein Cow

becomes a cow when she gives birth for the first time and freshens, or begins lactating.

For breeding purposes, Bonnie uses both artificial insemination (AI) and bulls. AI is safer because bulls can be aggressive and dangerous. However, AI is more intensive because the farmer must watch the cows carefully to determine exactly when they are in heat. When a cow is in heat, she gives off smells that induce the other cows to "ride" her.

Bonnie talked about "seasonality." She breeds their cows again two or three months after they give birth. Towards the end of gestation, she "dries" them out for about two months before they freshen again. This practice is good for the cows and gives Bonnie a two-month vacation from milking.

"Our farm is seasonal," she said. "Cows freshen—have their calves at the same time of year—spring for us—and I will dry them all up at the same time, so I can get a break as well. Our earth is cyclical. Why not us?"

Cows have a bell curve period of milk production. Their highest nutritional needs occur during the time of their highest milk production. Bonnie tries to match these needs with the time of best grass growth. She said this practice brings together the important factors needed for milk that is high in nutrients.

She went on to say that the milk from cows free to move around in the fresh air eating fresh grass has several health advantages over milk from cows that are confined in feedlots and fed rations formulated to produce more milk. The milk from grass-fed cows contains up to three times more Omega-3 fatty acid, which is the good fat the human body needs. Milk from grass-fed cows also contains up to five times as much conjugated linoleic acid (CLA), a nutrient that may reduce the risk of cancer and a number of immune disorders.

Pastured cows that do not receive rations formulated to produce more milk have more lactation periods before "burning out" than feedlot cows, which lactate only about 1 ½ to 3 times. Some of the cows that Bonnie started with were still giving milk. Feedlot cows, however, give more milk in each lactation period.

Unlike most feedlot dairies, PastureLand farmers do not use antibiotics, hormones, or grow genetically engineered crops. Consideration for the health of the land and wildlife plays an important role in all their practices. For example, on Springside Farm, there is no visible erosion; the dense grasses hold the soil in place even during heavy rains. Pastures interspersed with groves of trees offer a choice of sun or shade for the cows and provide habitat for wildlife, such as turkeys, deer, butterflies, birds, earthworms, fox and coyotes.

PastureLand members recognize the importance of local production and marketing. They have contracted with a small cheese factory that has produced a variety of cheeses from their milk, such as baby Swiss; mild, medium and sharp cheddar; plain and Cajun cheddar curds; and mild, medium and aged gouda in flavors of tomato/basil, herb/spice and dill. Pastureland cheeses appear in food co-ops, conventional grocery stores and on menus in restaurants in southeastern and western Minnesota and northeastern Iowa.

After feeding the calves, Bonnie and I continued our tour to the southern edge of the farm, where she showed me a long row of grass sealed in plastic. She explained that they do need to cut and bale some of their grasses. When they bale the grass wet and seal it in plastic, it pickles like silage, resulting in siled hay instead of corn. She also showed me a large rectangular mound, loosely covered in plastic, where winter feed of haylage and silage is already in the pasture, instead of in a silo.

On our way to visit the cows, Bonnie pointed out a structure that Vance retro-fitted into a reservoir for used water, which allows them to keep used and clean water separate. For this project, they received cost-share money from the Environmental Quality Incentive Program or EQIP. Vance similarly retro-fitted a milking parlor. Olaf, their 16-year-old son, keeps all the mechanisms in working order.

The cows were grazing in a paddock on the north side of the farm. When we reached them, Bonnie pointed out the Holsteins, which are black and white, and the crossbreeds of Holstein and Jersey, which are black, brown and white. She said they have some Beef, Ayreshire, Norwegian Red, New Zealand and Friesian Holstein genetics crossed in as well.

These cows stay outside in the fresh air all year long. On the windiest winter days, they get a choice of staying under cover. They prefer to be outside, unless the wind chill is too bad.

Bonnie opened one of the solar/earth-powered electric fences to move the cows into the next paddock, calling, "Come on girls, come on, come on, come on."

When they began walking towards us, she told me that each cow takes up to 33,000 bites a day. She said I should listen to them biting and chewing the grass. These are her favorite sounds on the farm. The sounds were comforting and hypnotic, like assurances from nature that she knows what she is doing.

Springfield farm is as complicated and simple as nature herself. Bonnie described her feelings about it to me.

"I farm the way I do because it makes sense," she said. "Cows are born grazers, good for the land when managed and requiring minimal equipment, time and cost. I thought this would be an economic way I could blend my home/family life with values of sustainable farming. Taking care of the land in a non-eroding manner with minimal use of chemicals, fuel and machinery, while adding to the food system is a style I can be proud of. I care about people. Food is a necessary part of our living. This is my contribution to society."

Birds, People
and Domestic Cats

Domestic cats kill two to three billion wild birds each year in the United States alone. These cats, along with habitat destruction and pesticide-induced reproductive failure, comprise the greatest threats to birds worldwide. Because they are popular pets and have no natural predators, their numbers continue to grow. There are at present about 60 million pet cats and 60 million feral cats (domestic cats gone wild) in this country.

The Kaffir cat (*Felis libica*), indigenous to North Africa, Turkey, India and the Mediterranean, is the main progenitor of our present day domestic cat. It was domesticated around the year 2500 BC by the Egyptians who used it to control the rats that plagued their granaries.

As the human population increased throughout the world, so did the rat population. Wherever man went and prospered, so did rats. Rats followed historic invasions, voyages of exploration and commercial trade routes. They brought the bubonic plague and contributed to famine by devastating grain stores. As his only defense against the rat, man introduced the domestic cat wherever he went.

In the United States, the domestic cat now plays the role of pet more often than rat exterminator. I have had cats in my home for 25 years. I love them for their purr, their size (perfect for a lap), grace of movement, the way they refuse to walk a straight line and their inscrutability.

I still wonder where Max, my golden tabby, went when he sat in front of a blank wall staring. What inner landscape did he inhabit?

I love the way my cats talk to me in a language halfway between meows and customary human speech. I love the way our body language allows us to meet somewhere between our two worlds.

Max used to read my intentions so well, he knew, almost before I did, when I planned to go away. I saw it in the way he held his head and looked up at me with his big yellow eyes. He knew when I was sad or anxious. His luxurious yellow body purring at my side or on my belly comforted me. He wouldn't leave me at these times. I'm not sure if it was from love or the anxiety of something not right in the world where we met.

All my cats have been adept at using their bodies to elicit desired human behavior. Without knowing how he got there, I would find Max on my lap, with my hand stroking his neck, feeling for the purr that told me I had it right. Limpy used to roll onto his back to announce he wanted his belly rubbed. Tim always got the treat he was meditating on when he sat Buddha-like facing our kitchen table, with his eyes squeezed shut, every time we had chicken for dinner. Nick, my untamed cat, flattens his ears when I try to touch him. Only when I bring him food does he allow me to scratch his head and sink my fingers into his silky black fur.

In their own world, a place we can learn about but cannot enter, cats communicate with each other through scent and marking behavior, visual displays, and a variety of vocalizations. They have a complex social system that includes a hierarchy and rules of etiquette.

These peeks into the general psychology of cats and the specific personalities of individual cats allow me to know how different and how similar they are to humans. My intimate knowledge of domestic cats links me to wild creatures, makes me want to know about them and teaches me how to go about doing so. I observe other species more carefully now. I notice sizes, colors, behaviors and habits of vocal and visual communication. I have observed and learned more about birds than any other wild creatures.

A useful way to understand the similarities and differences between humans and other species is by comparing our senses.

The common experience of vision provides an innate understanding between humans, cats, and birds, but the differences in the ways we see make certain that our experiences will never be exactly alike. When I looked at Max, I saw a pale gold cat with darker gold stripes. I recognized his face and could pick it out of a line-up of gold tabbies. When Max looked at me, he saw mostly movement. He didn't recognize my face, but knew the way I moved.

A wide range of visual ability exists among the various species of birds. Visual acuity, or the ability to distinguish detail, among hawks is about five times that of humans and 10 times that of cats. Nocturnal birds and cats have greater light gathering abilities than humans do. Day-flying birds see a color spectrum greater than humans do and much greater than cats. The only colors cats can see are blue, green, and possibly red.

Cats' whiskers give them a sense of touch people don't have, but both species relish back rubs. All mammals have hair, not only for warmth and protection but also for touching and grooming. Each hair has nerves around it, which convey tactile impulses to the brain.

Feathers also have tactile sensitivities, especially in the wing joints of birds, where they help govern wing positions in flight. Birds have strong tactile sensitivities to changes in atmospheric pressure and vibrations, allowing them to feel weather changes. Songbirds, for example, increase their vocalizations and feeding activity before a thunderstorm.

Acute hearing and a wide range of vocal abilities provide birds and humans with their primary means of communication. Humans hear a wider range of frequencies than birds. Some birds hear higher frequencies than people do. Some hear lower. Each species hears about the same range of sounds it can produce. Domestic pigeons hear infrasounds (very low frequencies) or vibrations made by meteorological and tectonic disturbances thousands of miles away.

Cats also have strong sensitivities to vibration and sound. They hear higher frequencies than humans and a wider range of frequencies than either humans or birds.

Much of a cat's social life involves marking behavior and responses to scent messages, indicating its sense of smell is its primary means of communication. A cat's sense of smell is so superior to ours that it's almost a different sense; it's a whole language.

My cats don't have as many taste buds as I do, but we all like the taste of fish. Birds generally have less developed senses of taste and smell than humans and cats.

Both birds and cats have extraordinary senses of balance and equilibrium that allow them to re-orient automatically with respect to gravity, even when blindfolded. Human senses of balance and equilibrium are far less acute.

When cats combine their sense of time with their sense of direction, they can navigate by the sun. They have physiological internal clocks set to home time that will not correspond to the sun's position in a place, say, 100 miles away. A computation of the time difference will give them the necessary directional cue and

Cat with White-throated Sparrow in its Mouth

allow them to find their way home. Birds also have internal clocks and navigate using the sun by day or the stars by night.

People and domestic cats are able to communicate more directly than people and wild birds. Humans have, however, through careful observation, learned the significance of certain avian vocalizations. In attempts to communicate, we call to birds by mimicking their language, or the calls of predators. Birds often respond vocally and with predictable behavior, but they are probably not responding to a person, only to the sound of another bird.

We have also learned the significance of avian visual displays, but visual communication between humans and wild birds is minimal. Some has to do with curiosity. Most has to do with perceived threats resulting in flight.

Direct communication may occur between feeder birds and their humans. I fill my feeders in the same order and at the same time every day. While doing so, I make twittering and whistling sounds. The little birds chatter in turn and flutter around my head. I think they recognize me as part of a whole picture, but wouldn't recognize me in a different context.

The most rewarding communication I have with birds is when I go deep into their world, mentally and physically, deep into the woods and wait. Eventually they come—chickadees, nuthatches, kinglets, and woodpeckers.

* * *

I said that my cats sparked my curiosity and gave me the tools to learn about creatures in the wild. I am not alone. One of the main reasons people have pets is for the link they provide to nature. Ironically, domestic animals and the people who breed them comprise an enormous threat to native wildlife.

I am a member of "MnBird," a Minnesota Birding Network. A recent discussion in this group concerned the predation of songbirds by domestic cats. It began with an ethical dilemma posed by a Duluth woman who had a neighbor that permitted her cat to be out of doors most of the time. The cat had taken up residence near the woman's feeders and had killed many birds. The woman asked if it was ethical for her to continue to feed birds in her backyard if they were being killed by the cat over which she had no control.

In response, some people attributed dishonorable traits to cats themselves. One man threatened to poison his neighbor's cats.

Some birders wrote in defense of the cat, as did I. Most wrote about their frustration with cat owners.

The root of the problem is not the cat acting according to its own nature. It is too many people with too many cats. The problem is always too many people. People-pressure destroys rain forests, fills in wetlands and creates toxic waste.

Our big brains come up with solutions that cause more problems. We create insecticides that destroy the predators who eat the insects that we want to destroy. We kill predators, then use guns to control an exploding deer population. We introduce cats to destroy rats, then complain of too many cats. Are we the plague raging across the planet?

The problem is not one cat owner who lets his cat go in and out at will. It is too many cat owners who allow their pets to roam. It is well-meaning people who feed birds in the territory of outdoor cats and loving cat owners who believe it is inhumane to spay or neuter their pets.

A major problem exists in rural areas with farmers who keep cats to control rodent populations, but don't recognize the need to control cat populations. When a cat population becomes too large for a farm to support, some of the cats wander into the countryside in search of food. I know this is true because several of those cats have found their way to my house.

I first found Max as a kitten, mewing on a stump in our backyard. Tim showed up one day and followed my husband around like a dog. Limpy arrived limping on a midwinter night that was 30 below zero. Nick enjoyed sunning himself under the bird feeders. We trapped him and brought him inside, where fear bounced him off the walls. It took years for him to make peace with his captivity. In exchange for a home, all our cats lost their freedom to roam and reproduce, although they are free to come and go on a fenced porch.

I consider myself a responsible cat owner, but I am also part of the problem. I don't have room in my home for all the stray and feral cats who wander into my yard, so I bang pots and pans to scare them away from my bird feeders, knowing that I am only sending them off to kill birds some place else. And if a kitten, a wounded or a skinny cat shows up when it's 30 below zero, nothing would stop me from feeding it. Not only that, I am not willing to give up the pleasure of feeding birds, which I know leads to unnatural concentrations which, in turn, attract more cats.

We humans have acted on our environment in so many obvious and subtle ways, we cannot hope to bring it back to a so-called natural state. We don't even know what that state is and guessing sometimes makes it worse.

I think the best we can do is strive for balance within the environment we have created for other creatures and ourselves. Extreme positions only add to the polarization of an already polarized society. Bird feeders are here to stay. Domestic cats are here to stay. Poisoning is neither a balanced nor an effective response to predation.

What is effective? Unfortunately, there is no easy or perfect solution. We can't get around the fact that to protect native wildlife, it is necessary to restrict the freedom and reduce the number of domestic cats. The first step is to convince cat owners of this necessity.

In urban areas, licensing and leash laws may be effective, if properly enforced. Conservation groups and bird clubs attempt to educate the public and the politicians. Humane societies and veterinary clinics work to convince pet owners that spaying and neutering are important tools in the prevention of the misery and destruction created by an exploding population of homeless pets.

In the end, the most effective tool will be the weight of public opinion. Progress will occur when widespread social mores dictate human responsibility. The responsibility is ours because we were the ones to domesticate cats.

Cats do not by nature destroy their environments. They become a problem only when man alters their genetics and moves them around the globe like pieces in a game of checkers.

Responsibility falls on us because we are different from the other animals. Not only are we capable of significantly altering our environment, we are capable of feeling guilt about our actions. The other animals do not experience guilt. They do not have ideas about right and wrong and what is ecologically sound.

Over the last 50 years, we have made extraordinary advances in our knowledge of what the environment is, what an organism is, and what a mind is. We have learned that, if we destroy our environment, we destroy ourselves.

We refer to the mind of nature and use words like ecosystem, ecology, systems theory, the Gaia Principle, sustainable development, holistic and community, but do we really understand what we are talking about? Are we as wise as we think? Our big brains still trick us into believing we can fool Mother Nature, that we can "fix" her with our clever technology. But, Nature's rules are strict and she is unforgiving.

Nature is greater than the sum of her parts and we are only parts having a difficult time thinking larger than ourselves. To predict the impact of our actions and understand nature's rules, we need to expand our boundaries to include ourselves-within-our-environment. This is not easy. It does not happen through force of will or technology. Different situations work for different people.

My boundaries expand when I go deep into the world of birds mentally and physically. I feel larger than myself when I find a cat on my lap, with my hand stroking his neck.

When I listen to a Beethoven symphony, or read Whitman's poetry, my edges blur and I have a feeling of clarity, a moment of knowing how the world works and an understanding that the artists who brought me here are still present and are experiencing the moment with me.

I long to stay in these moments, to be like the other animals, to experience the world through my entire being without self-consciousness, without analysis, without guilt, to be the organism that is myself-in-my-environment, but something always draws me back to the daily routines and the confines of my conscious self. Perhaps it is fear of losing my identity, without which I couldn't hear Beethoven, understand Whitman, or write this essay. Perhaps what draws me back is an urge to spread the word and to see what will happen next.

South Fork Bottomlands

I hear a soft
  chickadee-like sound and see
 a brown creeper disappear
  around a trunk near the
ground a hermit thrush slowly pumps
its rusty tail; each time it goes up,
I hear a low musical chuck.

My heart jumps when
a ruffed grouse explodes from the brush
still head high in places
dry leaves still on trees
rustle in a southwest wind
 an osprey struggles to fly against.

*American
Goldfinch on
Cow-Parsnip*

The sky is blue with a smear of white cloud.
Milkweed pods are spewing forth
another generation. A great blue heron
croaks and rises out of the stream
a bald eagle seems to follow.

A monarch rests on a milkweed
   stalk;
its orange and black wings
   move up and down
like the tail of a hermit thrush.
For a moment I see everything
   is in its place,
as always, the moment passes.

.

Monarch
Butterfly on
Milkweed

Porch with a View

It takes a lot to make me lose interest in birds, but one August that's exactly what happened. I knew the warblers were here. I could see them outside my open windows, as I lay on a couch nursing an injured back, desperately trying to find a comfortable position.

One day in early September, I decided to rig up a couch on my porch and watch fall migration from a reclining position. Although not ideal, it gave me an interesting perspective.

On pre-dawn mornings, I heard twitters of migrating birds, hoots of barred and great horned owls, cardinal clicks and robin calls. I saw shapes of warblers when it was still too dark to identify individual species. I saw the shadowy shapes of raccoons whistling and snuffling for acorns.

Early morning deer grazed in a field of wildflowers. When I spoke, they looked up as if to say, "Oh, it's only you," and then returned to their grazing. One morning, high metallic call notes alerted me to the presence of 30 rose-breasted grosbeaks.

In full morning light, I heard calls of yellow-bellied and least flycatchers, who offered long full views of their big heads on little bodies. Flickers and hairy woodpeckers shouted and bobbed up,

Blue-headed Vireo

down and around tree trunks. Sapsuckers imitated catbirds. Cedar waxwings flew in tight little flocks sparkling in the sun. One morning, 1,000 blackbirds streamed past my line of vision.

I learned a lot about an old bur oak that rises 75 feet into the sky, gently brushing the roof of my porch on its way up. Its leaves are like hands with large palms and stubby rounded fingers. The oak provides a home in a leaf, a city in a branch, a world to little birds shopping for food.

I saw 15 species of warblers in the oak. I was their captive audience, studying all the shades of Tennessees, Nashvilles and redstarts and the details of magnolias, chestnut-sided, bay-breasted, black and whites and Blackburnians.

I heard a low three-noted warble from an ovenbird, a blue-headed vireo's seven raspy mews and goldfinch babies begging for food. I noticed a pile of raccoon scat on a horizontal branch.

Every day around noon, I heard clicking sounds and saw cardinals dropping down to a small birdbath nestled among the trees. Then came chickadees, tufted titmice and rose-breasted grosbeaks, in all shades of development.

One day, three golden-winged warblers arrived at the birdbath together. On September 8, two Swainson's thrushes arrived and came every day for a couple weeks. Blue jays, never waiting for their turns, screeched in, scattering all the other birds. Between sips of water, they practiced their full repertoire of songs and calls. How can they produce all those sounds?

The afternoons were quiet, except for catbirds, black flies, and wind chimes. The evening show began at 4:00 p.m.

In late September, I began taking walks again, short ones at first. I drove short distances by car. I returned to the world of people and my old ways of watching birds from many points of view.

Raccoon

No Time – Only Cycles

Birds on this autumn morning are like a
symphony that gives hints of
what is to come and reminders of what has been.

The chestnut-sided warbler sings
a soft song hinting of past and future:
"pleased-pleased-pleased to meetcha."
The blue-winged warbler has a wider repertoire
in fall than spring,

yet is always his
   unmistakably
   buzzy self.
An immature
   titmouse offers
a reminiscence and
   prediction of
spring's loud and
   piercing "peter-
   peter-peter."

*Tufted Titmouse
in White Oak*

The leaves do it too, some still green
like summer,
some turned red and yellow,
some already on the ground forecasting
bare winter branches that are not really bare
if you look closely,
you will see a prediction of spring.

But, now I see the birds and leaves are not
like the symphony.
Beethoven, instead, got his ideas from them.

It's Not about a Yacht

Eagle
The eagle soars
no need for wing flapping
only an adjustment now and then
in her tail and the trim of her long black sails.

Some think sailing is only for the rich and young, but I know otherwise. My story takes place on Lake Pepin, a wide part of the Mississippi River between Minnesota and Wisconsin. It is the story of a lifetime dream for my husband. For me, it is a story of following the dreamer with whom I make my own dreams come true. It is the metaphor of a marriage. It is not about deep-water sailing, trips to the Caribbean, sailing around the world, or the America's Cup. It is not about a yacht. It has something to do with priorities, determination and desire.

On July 26, 1994, Art and I bought a used 17-foot sailboat in Chicago. We pulled the boat behind our 1977 Ford Maverick through rush hour Chicago, along Illinois highways, Wisconsin highways, Minnesota highways, county roads, township roads and up our steep gravel driveway.

The boat followed the car like a dog follows his best friend, but she looked incongruous sitting in the middle of our woods. We arranged for a berth at Hansen's Harbor on Lake Pepin, just north of Lake City, Minnesota. I considered taking sailing lessons from "Women in the Wind," because they promised gentle teachers and no yelling. Instead, I did what I usually do—I read a book and learned by doing.

On our first day of sailing, Art yelled at me. I cried and swore I'd never sail again. I should have taken those sailing lessons. Another day, the weather was stormy and we ran up against rocks. I was frightened and cried again. But I was determined to conquer my fear because I had felt the tug of the wind, the effect of the waves, the boat's response, my response and a sense of belonging I hadn't felt before.

In 1995, we bought "Running Free," a 22-foot Chrysler. Art convinced me it would be more seaworthy and easier to handle than our little boat. He was right, but I was still afraid in wind over 15 knots (about 17 miles).

By the end of the season, we had made some progress. No longer did others quake in terror and scramble to get out of the way as we clumsily maneuvered out of the harbor. No longer did our neighbors hear cursing and cries of, "I'll never sail again!" We had developed a routine and divided the tasks. I handled the tiller. He handled the sails and the motor.

* * *

The following are some excerpts from my sailing journal.

June 12: Southeast wind 15-25 knots. Pushing hard, we arrived at Lake City, seven miles downstream, tacking and reaching, gracefully high on our own abilities. Storm clouds were no deterrent.

Invincible, we sailed on. Wrong decision. The storm hit as I crouched on the deck dropping the sails. Art's scream was lost in the wind. I secured the sails and crawled into the cockpit. Rain drove silver needles into my skin. He revved the motor and tried to outrun the wind. It blew harder.

I grabbed the tiller and tried to steer.

He hollered, "We can't make it! Head for shore!"

The lake was black, invisible, then lit by a flash of light. Thunder roared. Monster waves lifted us up, then dropped us down.

Suddenly, the wind stopped and the sun came out. We raised our sails, drying them like cormorant wings.

July 20: We chased the perfect sail. A west wind of 10-20 knots came in gusts across the narrow lake, which meant there was not enough room to build up chops, although the waves showed some teeth. We passed Lake City on a beam reach. Then on a broad reach, we sailed toward Pepin Harbor.

Art said, "This is perfect, just what I wanted!"

As we heeled over, I felt the muscles in my arm match the resistance in the tiller.

Close to Pepin, we wore around and sailed back north. On a port tack moving fast, heeling over, our toes pressed into the starboard edge of the cockpit, the wind pulled us into herself. I couldn't pull the tiller any farther!

"We're over-powered!" I yelled. "Spill some wind from the mainsail, pull in the jib!"

We drove into the wind again! Too far! I heard the cleat release, the mainsail moved out, and we were back on course. It was time to tack, no time to think, only time to act or run aground. The wind whistled through the rigging, escalated, screeched, then stopped. Then began again.

We were a third of the way back to the harbor, heading up the lake on beam and close reaches. My neck was stiff and my toes were numb. My right arm twitched from the powerful resistance of the wind, the tiller and the weather helm. My eyes were fixed in the wind.

"She's handling it well," he said. I agreed.

We sailed on without talking. I felt the adjustments he made in the trim as he watched the wind and my hand on the tiller. I knew he was watching me. He was afraid I would panic. I had done it before. A picture of a glass of wine flashed through my mind.

The wind let up, giving us time to think, time for a sip of water before she hurled herself against us again, not to get even, no intention, merely a force. She carried us then straight to the harbor. I put the boat in irons. Art pulled in the jib and took down the main.

As we motored into port, our neighbor asked, "What's it like out there?"

"Lively," we replied, "a good day for sailing."

July 21: Southwest wind 15-30 knots, partly cloudy, a threat of rain, high 70s. The wind at home whipped the trees and blew an ashtray off our kitchen table. Art wanted to sail. Not wanting to show my fear, I went along.

The flags in Winona flapped and slapped erratically, and a small lake had whitecaps. Lake Pepin didn't look as angry as I had expected, but there were only five or six boats out.

Our neighbor said, "It's windier than yesterday, but you'll be okay." We reefed our mainsail one point.

Art said, "Pepin Harbor or bust!" I held my tongue.

Suddenly he yelled, "It's too much. Turn down wind. I'm going to reef the jib!"

I yelled back, "Don't reef too much. We need the drive!" I knew if we reefed too much the jib would flap and luff.

After Central Point, which was as rough as usual, we sailed smoothly into the wind on a starboard tack.

I called out, "Pepin or bust! Don't spill so much wind. Let's do this right."

The wind let up then came across the lake again, dark and foreboding. I watched and waited a year or two. We couldn't turn back. We were too close to shore to wear around. Crack! The sails whipped out. We heeled to 40 degrees. Crack! went the keel as she flipped out of the water and slapped back in.

We reached Pepin Harbor at 4:00 p.m. A monster thunderhead rose in front of us. We waved at other sailors and wore around to sail back north on a broad reach, wind on our port.

"The wind is dying down," he said. "It's not pushing us as hard as yesterday."

We relaxed and ate our lunch. We didn't watch our backs. We didn't see the wind and roiling waves rushing up behind. Suddenly, we were whipped around, blown on our side. I fought for control and was losing the fight as Art struggled to release the sails. Snap! went the cleat. We were back on course, with renewed respect for the forces that make sailing as serious as it is fun.

September 5: Southeast wind 5-15 knots, humid, hazy, mid 80s. The wind looked stronger than forecast so we threw binoculars, bird book, boat keys, crackers and two plums into the green basket, fed the cats an extra treat, and we were on our way.

On Lake Pepin, the waves showed their teeth. We reefed the main one point. The wind confused us, sent us north, then south. We sailed smooth and fast, then stopped. A small boat almost ran into us. We yelled to alert its crew as we veered off downwind, losing our momentum. The wind picked up again and the small boat followed us like a tin can tied to a tail as we tacked back and forth across the point.

The wind died. We shook out our full main and Genoa sail. The air was humid. The lake looked like molten lead, almost solid. Feeling like the "Ancient Mariner," we headed downwind. It was late. It was hot. Shadowy outlines of other boats disappeared and reappeared in the murky haze. Just as we dropped the sails to motor back, we saw the white foam of waves rising behind us again.

October 10: Southwest wind, 10-20 knots, sunny, 60 degrees. We sailed with a full main and working jib on close and beam reaches to Pepin Harbor. When we sailed well, we felt proud of our skill.

Some situations we didn't understand, like when we moved smoothly on a port tack and only minutes later poorly on a starboard tack. It might have been due to misreading the wind, trying to point too high, the shape of our sails, the shape of the lake, the positions of valleys and bluffs, all of these things, or something we didn't realize.

This is the ecology of sailing, of learning a skill. It begins with learning in school, reading books, or by watching someone else. Then comes practice, making the skill part of who you are, imprinting it on your brain. Soon you no longer consciously think about each little step you must take. You no longer consciously know what you know. And you don't know what it is you have yet to learn, only that there is always something more.

What had we learned? We had learned to trust our boat, how to make minute adjustments in the tiller by the way it felt in our hands, how to trim the sails to fit the wind, how to watch the lake and wait for the calm before the storm.

What did we have yet to learn? We couldn't say exactly, but we knew it was much when we watched the eight other boats sailing that day, all doing better than we were. And we knew we would never be as good as the South Sea Islanders, who learned to propel their canoes by the feel in their testicles.

As we wore around and headed back north, a good south wind sent us directly back to port. The Hansen's Harbor men were busy pulling boats out of the water. It was time to put "Running Free" away for the season.

Lars

On October 27, 1998, Edwin and Marcella Larson of LaCrosse, Wisconsin notified area birdwatchers of a strange hummingbird at their feeder. It was a shimmering green with violet patches behind its eyes. Fred Lesher and Dennis Kuecherer of LaCrosse, the first visitors to see the bird, identified it as a male green violet-ear, whose normal range is Mexico and Central America.

Word of this rare sighting spread quickly. Over the next several days, the Larsons opened their home to 250 people who came to see the little hummer, now called Lars. At first, I wondered if anyone besides me was concerned about the bird's welfare. If this little guy was so far from home, something was certainly wrong. Were people coming just to check off another species on their life lists?

I soon learned that Fred and Dennis had considered Lars's welfare from the beginning. They knew he would be in trouble as the days grew colder, so they contacted Marge Gibson, a medical avian biologist and International Director for Rehabilitation of Avian Species in Antigo, Wisconsin. The plan was to capture the bird, transport him to Marge for rehabilitation, and then fly him to hummingbird biologists in Corpus Christi, Texas.

Messages of concern and advice flowed in from 17 states and three foreign countries as people continued to visit Lars, who was becoming weaker every day. When Gene Bauer of Northfield, Minnesota arrived on Sunday morning, October 31, Lars was nowhere to be seen, an almost certain sign he had perished the night before. Then, as a small group of people mourned the little bird, Lars appeared one last time.

Green Violet-ear

Gene wrote about this moment: "The green violet-ear fluttered bush-high from the north side of the house and fell to the lawn, wings spread, its body shaking. Tom [Tom Schultz, of LaCrosse, illustrator of the new Peterson guide to warblers] walked past me out the door, to the feeder, and in a gesture that seems a symbol of all we are or can be, he offered the warmth and protection of his hand."

The group quickly prepared the hummer for a three-hour drive with Dennis and Fred to Marge Gibson's rehabilitation center. When they arrived in Antigo, Marge was ready with fluids, protein massages, a steroid shot, antibiotics and vitamins, all for one small creature 4 ¾ inches long.

Sue Levy, of St. Paul, probed the decisions leading to heroic measures to save Lars. She questioned the value of using funds to save just one bird and asked if the money shouldn't go instead to improve habitats for many birds.

My husband Art wrote a response to Sue's questions that seemed to speak for all of us: "I know why we want to save the little hummer. Because he has touched our hearts. We had no choice. The glittering little jewel from far away touches us as the face of a small child in need touches us. We are captured and held prisoners of his innocence and need. Finally, in the depths of the night, we know we can't accept a world that can find no compassion for the least of God's creatures."

Marge informed us of Lars's condition every step of the way. On Sunday night, November 1, she reported that he had improved since his arrival earlier in the day. On Monday, Lars was perky and aware of Marge for the first time. Tuesday was his best day yet. By Tuesday evening, he had balance problems and showed signs of infection. On Wednesday, his lungs were filling. On Thursday, November 5, Marge wrote that little Lars had finally grown tired and had quietly slipped away.

The U.S. Fish and Wildlife Service chose to send his body to the Bell Museum at the University of Minnesota for examination and preservation. Since there are no other records of a green violet-ear reported in the Northern Hemisphere, it was important that Lars go to a place with superior capabilities. The Bell Museum has state-of-the-art facilities and two internationally known ornithologists, Dr. Robert Zink and Dr. Scott Lanyon, both of Minneapolis.

Lars had achieved some measure of immortality, not only in the preservation of his body, but in the hearts of those he touched. Now, whenever I see harshness or cruelty, I remind myself that compassion is also part of the human psyche, as witnessed by the response to a little Mexican hummingbird with the unlikely name of Lars.

Hunting Season

I always dread deer hunting season, when the woods rings with the sound of guns and the complaints of crows and blue jays. When we first moved to the Big Woods, Art hunted, but living in such close proximity to other creatures soon caused him to change his mind. He preferred to watch the creatures rather than kill them.

I have always disliked hunting. My dad was a hunter and fisherman and I never enjoyed looking at his proudly-displayed catches.

I don't like suffering. When I see it, I suffer too. I carry wasps out of the house in paper towels and let spiders spin where they will. However, I am willing to kill certain living things without even thinking about it, such as flies and mosquitoes. And I eat meat. Is the difference between a hunter and me only a matter of degree?

Although I judge my fellow man all the time, I don't judge other animals that kill. I watched a sharp-shinned hawk kill a cardinal and saw no moral component to this graceful, even beautiful, act.

My dad was not a cruel man and neither are most hunters.

So, in an effort to understand what draws people to this activity, I decided to compare hunting with my methods of pursuing wildness.

I love learning all there is to know about birds. I learn their habits. I read their tracks. My heart pounds and my breath comes fast as I stalk my prey. I feel a sense of accomplishment and belonging in a natural order where communication has nothing to do with words. In this way, I am a hunter too.

* * *

Early one evening, as I walked down my driveway, I heard coyotes howling and footsteps approaching. My rational self said

Ruffed Grouse and Jack-in-the-Pulpit

I wasn't in danger, but my heart told me otherwise. I turned and walked home as fast as I could. I was afraid to run.

I want this experience again, the adrenaline, the primal fear of being hunted. Do hunters also seek this kind of exhilaration?

* * *

Although I hate the sound of guns and the suffering it implies, death itself fascinates me. A ruffed grouse hit our window. I picked it up and held it close. I felt its heart beat, then stop. At that moment, the bird in my hands grew smaller and, as it diminished in physical size, it seemed to permeate the woods. Is there a desire to be close to the event of death? Is there some irresistible urge to come face to face with mortality?

* * *

Every fall, I go to Riecks Lake at Alma, Wisconsin, to watch the tundra swan migration. I nod to other watchers as I walk along the shore. I stand silently beside people I've never seen before and may never see again. Words cannot explain what draws us here. Words are not necessary. Do hunters experience this kind of camaraderie?

Like me, hunters also play important roles in preservation of habitat. Maybe we can co-exist peacefully after all. I just have a few requests. Please aim carefully, shoot to kill, don't let a wounded creature get away only to suffer. Don't shoot from your car or too close to my house. Don't hunt in large groups or throw deer parts on the sides of roads. Please leave the beer at home. Please respect our "no hunting" signs and watch out for me walking in the woods. I'll be wearing my blaze orange vest.

Christmas Servive
in Pioneer Church

Heat from the 5-foot tall wood stove stung our faces and made us shed jackets and sweaters. We had arrived at the last minute and the only remaining places to sit were next to the stove. I hadn't expected to see such a crowd in the little Lenora United Methodist Church, the oldest church in Fillmore County.

It was December 23, 2000, a clear cold evening, 10 degrees below zero. Rev. Mark Woodward, pastor of Faith United Methodist Church of Eyota, Minnesota, had opened the pioneer church in the small settlement of Lenora, five miles north of Canton, for a Christmas service. Rev. Woodward serves this church out of his interest in history, evangelism and Christian outreach.

The church was built in 1856 and rebuilt in 1865 after the Civil War. It is made of limestone rock and is approximately 24 feet wide by 30 feet long.

Its first pastor was circuit rider Rev. John Dyer, who had moved to the Lenora area in 1856 with his three sons and a daughter. He had raised money to build the church by selling small parcels of his own 40 acres, thus creating the town of Lenora.

Lenora's first post office opened in 1856 in Elija Austin's home, with Charles B. Milford postmaster. It later moved to the general store, where it remained until closing for good in 1905. Rev. Dyer's son Joshua opened the first store. The town also had a doctor and a hotel.

The first religious camp meeting in the area took place on June 3, 1856, before the church was built. The meeting drew between 1,500 and 2,000 people and lasted more than a week. Preachers at the meeting included Elder Norris Hobart, Reverends Dyer and Benjamin Crist and Brothers Willford, Bissel, Johnson and Phelps. During the meeting, all seven men preached at the same time from seven different crudely erected pulpits.

After leaving Lenora, Rev. Dyer served in Caledonia, Austin and Wabasha and eventually moved to Colorado where he made a name for himself as a pioneer preacher. Many preachers served in Lenora after Rev. Dyer. Some of them were circuit riders who traveled from community to community, never staying long in one place.

When the railroad passed it by in the late 1800s, the once lively town began to decline. By the late 1920s, the pioneer church no longer had an active congregation.

The Lenora Cemetery Association and the Newburg United

*Lenora United
Methodist Church*

Methodist Church cared for the little church over the years and kept it from falling into total disrepair. Today, with the help of Rev. Woodward, it is open to the public again as a historical landmark, for monthly services from June to October, and for special services throughout the year.

While waiting for the Christmas service to begin on that cold evening of December 23, 2000, we had time to look around the little church. A Christmas tree with red bows stood near the pulpit. Wreaths hung in the six window alcoves. Oil lamps on the windowsills, walls and in a chandelier lighted the church. A threadbare American flag with 44 stars hung on the wall behind the pulpit. A refurbished Story and Clark reed organ stood to the right of the pulpit. All 25 pews were filled to capacity.

Rev. Woodward generated a feeling of camaraderie with his opening words. The feeling intensified as we sang "Joy to the World." We were all casually dressed, but it was not hard to envision a 19th century congregation of women and girls in bonnets and long skirts and men and boys in dark suits. One could almost hear their loud clear voices singing Christmas carols. Outside, horses and buggies would have been awaiting the return of their families.

Rev. Woodward was reading a scripture passage when he suddenly stopped and called out, "Harold, are you okay?"

An elderly gentleman sitting near the center of the church had slumped over in the pew. Perhaps he had only fallen asleep, but he was not responding to the questions anxiously directed at him. When he finally did respond, he appeared disoriented, but, with help was able to walk to the door. Four nurses came to his aid and someone ran to a nearby house to call 911.

While Rev. Woodward remained at Harold's side, another visiting pastor continued the church service. Offering up a little fire and brimstone, he told us we must prepare for judgment day.

Every once in awhile we looked anxiously to where Harold waited at the back of the church. We sang more songs, heard more scripture passages and listened to the music of a trumpet and two flutes.

Then we heard a commotion at the back of the church and soon Rev. Woodward returned to tell us that the Harmony Ambulance had come to take Harold to St. Mary's Hospital in Rochester. He said it looked as if Harold would be all right.

We sang the last Christmas carol, "Silent Night," with great feeling and camaraderie deepened by the shared anxiety and subsequent relief for a fellow worshipper.

Most of us had never met before, but it seemed as though we knew each other as we shook hands, said our Merry Christmases and filed back out into a cold December night that suddenly didn't feel so cold.

Ice Storm

Three days after an ice storm, the ice melting from the trees sounded like rain. The next day everything was again frozen solid. Ice-covered branches rattled in a slight breeze. Chickadees sang. Woodpeckers drummed.

The gravel road was slippery. The township had sanded it, but the thaw from the day before had sucked the sand into pools of water that froze again the next day.

Footing was easiest on the roadside, where tufts of brush poked through ice. I stood on ice while following a titmouse with my binoculars. Suddenly my feet went out from under me. Soon I would be nursing a bruised hip. Could have been worse. Could have broken a bone.

I crossed the icy bridge by holding onto its red iron railing. The bridge crosses the South Fork of the Root River, which was the only thing flowing in that frozen world.

A loud high-pitched call and an answer almost made me fall again. Suddenly, long black wings and a flashing white head and tail rose out of a tree just above my head. It looked like the eagle wouldn't be enjoying a trout dinner just yet.

Red-tailed Hawk

I pulled my journal and waterproof cushion out of my back-pack and sat by the stream. A belted kingfisher zoomed rattling down the stream.

* * *

The next day, I made my way down woodland paths to the South Fork. The paths were almost as slippery as the roads had been. A thin layer of hard white ice covered fallen logs. I could see through the ice to the bark. The sounds of a chainsaw and a falling tree split the silence.

At the water's edge, I saw a rock in the shape of a hawk. Then I saw it had feathers. Was it still breathing? I stroked a downy belly, spread reddish tail feathers to their full buteo width and touched an ice crystal like a tear under its eye. I couldn't help thinking of the box of skinned muskrats I had found in the same spot a year earlier.

The chainsaws were suddenly quiet. My thoughts turned to the previous fall, when I had hiked to a nearby wooded valley, another of my favorite walking places and a good place to look for birds. On that day, I had heard the whine of chainsaws and had looked into a bare sky, instead of into trees.

I had stopped to talk with the owner of the land, a hard-working dairy farmer, family man and good neighbor, who had once pulled me out of a huge snowdrift on a blustery sub-zero day.

"There's lots of good timber in this valley," he said. "Time to put it to use."

Returning from my thoughts to the dead hawk, I smoothed its red tail feathers, stroked its soft belly one last time and climbed into the bluffs through crowns of trees left lying across the trail. Bare sky appeared in place of the forest canopy.

I passed the cliff and the cave where I used to sit 300 feet above the valley floor. While there, I always tried not to disturb the birds and other creatures, but knew even my quiet presence had an effect.

Suddenly, the chainsaws started up again. It looked like lunch hour was over.

When I reached the field bordering my land, I found dozens of trees, their heads and feet cut off, spread out in a mass grave. The lumbermen were cutting everything over a foot in diameter. I waved to the workers, but didn't stop to talk.

Finally, I was back in my own woods. While standing still on an icy deer trail, my feet went out from under me. I picked myself up and limped towards the house. Chickadees, nuthatches and cardinals seemed to accompany me, but I knew they were only on their way to the feeders. A large black bird soared in the distance. Through binoculars, I saw a pure white head.

The sounds of chainsaws and a falling tree cracked the frozen air.

The Cave

It was a warm autumn day. A tree branch arched over the old tractor trail that I had first traveled almost 30 years earlier in a mule-drawn wagon with Bobby and Phyllis Norby. Its twists and turns over the years remained about the same in my eyes, but it was changing all the time. A fallen branch may have changed its course. Erosion played a part.

On that autumn day, the trail led through trees with leaves still green, some turning yellow and orange. The sun shone in patches. A light wind played with sun and shadow. A chipmunk scratched in dry leaves, filling his cheeks with acorns. A ruffed grouse fanned his tail and stepped deliberately past my line of vision.

I arrived at the cave, which is actually only a hollow place in rock on a bluff that seems to guard the South Fork. I had been going there for years to sort through the stubborn problems of my life.

* * *

On another autumn day in a different year, clouds sailed past like fleets of ships. It was a good day for a walk, if you kept moving. I arrived at the cave and sat there sheltered from the wind.

The tin can was still rusting in its usual place, as it had ever since I had been going there. Nothing had changed much, as far as I could tell.

Ten minutes earlier, I had been sitting on the ground by the South Fork. Robins called in the trees on the opposite bank. They flew one by one in a stream to the water's edge, then back into the trees. I heard them as they dropped down, their wings making sounds like rain or wind across dry leaves.

Cedar waxwings had risen out of the trees, one small flock, then another and another, as though the trees were giving birth. Each flock flew as a single entity with no apparent leader, no individual making decisions.

A robin had chased a flicker. Chickadees and nuthatches had appeared and a gray squirrel came running down a path through the grass. I could tell he was accustomed to the path. When he reached the water, he drank, then jumped to the branch of a tree hanging across the stream. I looked through binoculars and saw him watching me. When I took a step in the dry leaves, he flicked his tail and scampered across the tree to the opposite bank.

* * *

One winter day, the snow had melted enough on our woodland trails to allow a walk down to the South Fork. A pickup truck stood in the path up to the cave. The only sounds I could hear were the stream flowing, an airplane droning, and a caw. I wondered where the driver of the truck was, who he was—a trapper, a hunter, a walker in the woods like me?

No words came to me while I sat on a log waiting for inspiration. No squirrels, no birds. I walked to the pickup truck. A box of bullets sat on its bed. Inside the cab, I saw a blaze orange case for a gun. What was he hunting? Deer season was over, I thought.

I looked up and there he was, sitting on a rock near the cave in blaze orange, a gun across his lap. Soon the orange man came down the path.

"Where's your blaze orange?" he asked. "Don't you know there are deer hunters here? I thought I should warn you. I don't want you to get hurt."

* * *

On another winter day, it was 35 degrees and breezy. Not many birds were visible, but I could hear the calls of crows, jays, a flicker and the tap-tap-tapping of chickadees. The gray squirrel was there in the valley below the cave. He was on his way to the South Fork through the treetops. He stopped, chattered twice, flicked his tail and moved on.

The tin can still rusted in the cave. Icicles hung like protective bars before her opening. They formed drip by slow drip; each drop elongated, formed a jewel at its tip, and finally dropped.

* * *

One spring day, I picked my way down the muddy path through our property to the South Fork. When I reached the creek, I saw trout flinging themselves into the air, breaking water into silver pieces. A tufted titmouse sang. A muskrat swam into a bank I

*Gray Squirrel
on White Oak*

didn't know had a hole. Dragonflies darted.

The air was busy with flycatching ruby-crowned kinglets and yellow-rumped warblers. A winter wren sang, while fussing among rocks and roots at a bend in the stream that is 6 feet across. Swamp sparrows foraged deep in the brush.

I turned to go home up the old tractor trail to the cave where the trees have been cut down. The cave and the tin can were still there, but nothing else looked the same.

*Cedar Waxwings
in Red Cedar*

Nancy

It was the middle of April. Four inches of snow had fallen overnight. More snow threatened. The Big Woods road was sloppy. It was easiest to walk in the tire tracks.

I wondered how the birds were faring in the winter-like weather. Some of the bug eaters, such as phoebes, robins, bluebirds, song sparrows and red-winged blackbirds had already arrived. When I reached the bridge, I saw the first yellow-rumped warbler of the season.

The sky looked threatening. It began to snow again. I decided not to go off the road into the woods. I would walk as far as Rosheim Hill, then turn around. Three vultures were circling overhead. What were they watching?

A car drove up behind me and stopped. "What are you seeing?" asked my friend Nancy.

She knew I was looking for birds. I told her about the warbler at the bridge. "The herons are here," she said. "Have you seen the eagle lately?"

"I saw it fly down the river this morning," I replied. "What do you think of this gloomy spring?"

"It makes me restless," she said. "I shouldn't be driving with another storm coming, but I had to get out."

Nancy and Jack lived two miles from us, down the road, across the bridge, then to the right at the "Y". They had designed their earth-sheltered house themselves. The South Fork of the Root River bordered their yard.

"I can't wait to get my hands in the dirt again," Nancy said.

Every year, she planted several vegetable and flower gardens. Jack tended a small vineyard near their barn. When Nancy and Jack first moved here from Minneapolis, they had opened Mrs. B's, a bed and breakfast in Lanesboro.

Lanesboro sits in a valley in the middle of bluff country. The Root River runs through it. Mrs. B's received widespread publicity and gave other entrepreneurs the incentive to begin tourist-centered businesses in Lanesboro and nearby towns. Nancy and Jack eventually sold their business to spend more time on their land.

Great Blue Heron

"I've been feeling a little down," I said, "but I'll be all right once I can get back into the woods."

We talked about the power of the forest, how it offers perspective, how it gives us hope and shows us that something is right in the world. We often talked like this during our chance encounters. We had always shared a neighborly sort of intimacy.

It began to snow harder. The wet heavy snow was building up on my head and shoulders and making my teeth chatter, so I reluctantly ended our conversation and made my way home.

One Spring

Spring is a time of urgency for me, of feeling that I mustn't miss the first swelling pussy willows, the first blooming hepatica, the first robin, or yellow-rumped warbler. I want to walk fast because I have so much energy, because I see so much energy around me—in the birds constantly singing with nothing but sex on their minds, in wildflowers unfolding before my eyes. But, to watch a robin or a phoebe building a nest, I must walk slowly or stop altogether.

I must admit I can't see it all, but in stopping to watch the phoebe, I know that, in a way, I am seeing all of spring, all springs merging into one.

When I began my walk one spring day, the air felt soft on my skin. A spider's web glinted in the sun between the railings of my new front porch. Spring beauties bloomed in my yard.

At the curve of my driveway, I stopped by an area of brush kept low for the power line. A blue-winged warbler was perched on the line singing. He sings all spring, every spring.

The year before, I had come upon two fledglings there. They still had downy feathers, wide gapes, short tails and were barely able to fly from twig to twig in the low brush. I wouldn't have known they were blue-winged warblers without seeing their two agitated parents hovering nearby.

A field sparrow also sings in this area all spring and summer long and rose-breasted grosbeaks nest in the nearby prickly ash.

Around the curve, my driveway cuts into a hill on one side and drops off to a sheltered hollow on the other. One year, a turkey laid 10 eggs on the ground in the hollow and a ruffed grouse nested on the side of the hill. The nests and eggs still exist in my mind.

As I continued my walk, I noticed hepatica were blooming along

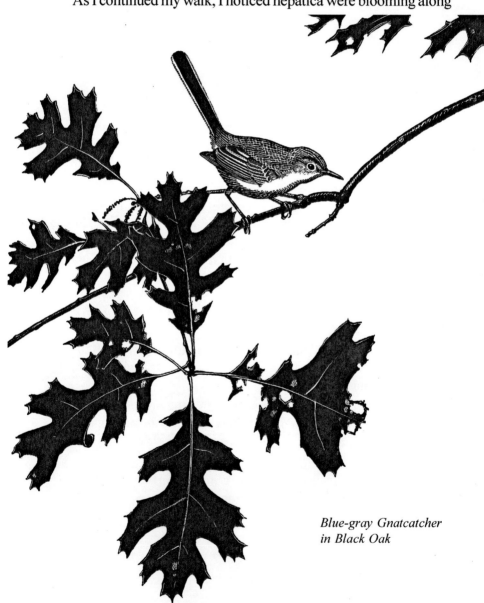

Blue-gray Gnatcatcher
in Black Oak

the driveway, bloodroot leaves were up and fiddleheaded ferns had risen out of the ground.

Sixty feet high in a basswood tree, a pair of blue-gray gnat-catchers was flitting around decorating the outside of their tiny nest with bits of lichen. I had first seen them 10 days earlier, building their nest of plant down, fibers and catkins, held together by spider silk.

When I reached our mailbox and the culvert at the entrance to our driveway, I thought about the time many years ago when Amherst Township installed the culvert after we had almost lost our new Chevy pickup in the ditch. Neighbors and township commissioners, with hands in their pockets and seed caps on their heads, had come to watch the installation.

As I turned on to the Big Woods Road, I waved to my Amish neighbors, who passed me in their horse-drawn buggy on their way to church.

To my left, high in a young elm, I saw a redstart nest; it rivals the gnatcatchers' in beauty and delicacy of construction. American redstarts nest in this tree or a neighboring tree every year. One year I had witnessed the whole process: nest building, incubation, feeding of the nestlings and finally feeding of the fledglings.

I paused at the spring that supplied our water before we had a well. It forms a small run that drains into the South Fork. Northern cardinals, tufted titmice, ovenbirds, scarlet tanagers, indigo buntings and yellow-throated vireos have nested in this area. Solomon's seal and a patch of ginger grow here every summer.

Just before the South Fork bridge, I came to the house where Rueben lived with his son Pancake when we moved to the Big Woods in 1978.

On the opposite side of the road, the Mogers had a campfire burning, country western music playing and ATV's running. Martin Ackerman was there, too, drawing water from Mogers's well.

By then, Brenda had moved to Rochester with her daughter. Her four sons, almost grown, were still with their father.

A couple years earlier, Martin had said to me, "Gonna get electricity this year. Don't want to spend another winter in Harmony. It was them hoodlums from Harmony broke into Mogers's place. Tore it apart."

I waved to the people at Mogers's and moved on. When I

reached the bridge, I heard the whistling of cedar waxwings and could still see three of their nests from the year before. At least six species of warblers were singing there, including a Louisiana waterthrush. But, warbler migration isn't like it used to be. I remember seeing waves of warblers with up to 15 species every day of spring. That hasn't happened for many years now.

Other changes have occurred in the Big Woods since we moved here. We have seen the building and demolishing of houses and barns. Residents have come and gone.

The Amish, who arrived about the same time we did, have grown in numbers. The countryside is dotted with their graceful white houses. They have left their marks on the Big Woods in other ways. They built Bratrud's barn and recycled a house on Erik and Kathy Erickson's property. Up the road from Erickson's are Heidi and Phil Dybing who took over where Houskers left off, remodeling and adding to the house.

Over the years, Big Woods children have become adults and parents have become grandparents. The Norby clan continues to grow. Gardens and lawns have appeared; some have returned to woods. Most of us have electricity and running water now.

As I looked into the South Fork from the bridge, I noticed a

school of brown trout. Generations of trout have come and gone over the years, but their colors are always the same and trout season still opens every April.

Beyond the bridge, I came to the stump where chickadees were excavating a nest and the place where Joe-Pye-weed grows. Great spangled fritillaries were flying in the small meadow there. Red admiral butterflies were everywhere. A few tiger swallowtails and a mourning cloak floated by.

To my right was the road to Bratrud's house. Nancy and Jack were busy packing. They had sold their home and were about to forsake the Big Woods for Duluth.

I paused again at the big curve in the road and the secluded place where brook

Wild Turkeys

trout have been swimming for as long as I can remember. Around the curve, I stopped to check on the yellow warbler nest that I had found a few days earlier built between stalks of cow parsnips.

At first, I had thought the nest was too big for the small birds. Then I realized it was one complete nest on top of another. In checking my references, I had found that these birds will build a second nest in this manner if a cowbird lays an egg in the first.

Beyond the warbler nest, I came to the place where a rotting tree once fell across the road at my feet and a family of flying squirrels had scampered out. Their strange appearance had scared me at first.

Between the flying squirrel place and Rosheim Hill are more animal trails, a walnut grove, a wild raspberry patch, a red-tailed hawk's nest and a secret gate that leads to the source of Blagsvedt Run. Mercy Valley Farm has replaced the old Rosheim farm, but we still drive up Rosheim Hill.

On my way back home, I saw two red-tailed hawks sunning themselves in a tree high on the bluff. When I stopped to get a better look, they lifted their great wings and flew out of sight. A cardinal sang "wheet-cheer" and a chickadee sang "spring's here." The birds still sing the same songs they've always sung, but there are fewer of them now.

Since we moved to the Big Woods, our trees have grown. Some have fallen and new trees have taken their places. But, many of the trees in the Big Woods have been cut for lumber. It will take more than a century for new trees to grow as large.

I have changed, too, over the years. I have crows' feet now and gray hairs are getting easier to find. It's becoming harder to climb into the bluffs, but I still get up there once in a while. I am still passionate about birds and enjoy visiting with people I meet along the Big Woods road.

When I reached the curve of my driveway again, I saw a rose-breasted grosbeak carrying nesting material.

Bibliography
& Credits

Credits

The following essays appeared in different versions in the *Fillmore County Journal* (Preston, MN).

Rueben
The Workshop
Possessed
At Home in the Woods
Doc Risser
The Great Bird Day
Going Underground
Habitat Improvement
Trout Opener
Yellow-bellied Sapsucker
Bluff Country Bird Festival
The Great Horned Owl of Houston
Survival
A Big Woods Wedding
Bird Survey at Hvoslef WMA

A House burning in the Big Woods
Green Lea Manor
Stella
Storm and Aftermath
Butterflies through Binoculars
Big Woods Celebrities
PastureLand
Crossing Cultures
It's Not about a Yacht
Lars
Hunting Season
Christmas Service in Pioneer Church

The following essays appeared in different versions in *Minnesota Birding*, The Minnesota Ornithologists' Union, Minneapolis, MN

Birds and the Ecology of Learning
Anne Marie
Doc Risser
The Great Bird Day
Habitat Improvement
Yellow-bellied Sapsucker
Migration Survey
Bluff Country Bird Festival
The Great Horned Owl of Houston
Big Woods Celebrities
Porch with a View
Carol
Ice Storm

Bibliography

Part I

Geologic Atlas, Fillmore County, Minnesota. St. Paul: University of Minnesota, 1995.

Bray, Edmund C. *Billions of Years in Minnesota, the Geological Story of the State*. St. Paul: Science Museum of Minnesota, 1985.

Dennett, Daniel C. *Darwin's Dangerous Idea; Evolution and the Meanings of Life*. New York: Touchstone, 1995.

Hvoslef, Johan C. *Dagbok 1*. 1881-1882. Unpublished. Minneapolis: University of Minnesota Archives; Elmer Andersen Library.

—. *Dagbok 2*. 1882-1883. Unpublished. Minneapolis: University of Minnesota Archives; Elmer Andersen Library.

—. *Diary 3*. 1904-1905. Unpublished. Minneapolis: University of Minnesota Archives; Elmer Andersen Library.

—. *Diary 10*. 1911-1912. Unpublished. Minneapolis: University of Minnesota Archives; Elmer Andersen Library.

Lewis, Mary. "Embarking." Unpublished, 2001.

Lusardi, B.A. *Minnesota at a Glance; Quaternary Glacial Geology*. St. Paul: University of Minnesota, 1997.

Roberts, T.S. *The Birds of Minnesota*. Minneapolis: The University of Minnesota, 1932.

Runkel, A.C. *Minnesota at a Glance; Ancient tropical seas—Paleozoic History of Southeastern Minnesota.* St. Paul. University of Minnesota, 2000.

Skutch, Alexander. *A Naturalist on a Tropical Farm.* Berkeley: University of California,1980.

Skutch, Alexander. *The Minds of Birds.* College Station: Texas A&M, 1996.

Part II

Bauer, Gene. Posting to *MnBird@*linux2.Winona.msus.edu, 31 Oct. 1999.

Fox, Michael W. *Understanding Your Cat.* New York: Coward, McCann & Geoghegan, 1974.

Gill, Frank B. *Ornithology.* New York: W.H. Freeman and Company, 1995.

Glassberg, Jeffrey. *Butterflies through Binoculars; the East.* Oxford, NY: Oxford University, 1999.

Hmong Lives; from Laos to LaCrosse, compiled and translated by Wendy Mattison, Laotou Lo, and Thomas Scarseth. LaCrosse, WI: The Pump House, 1994.

Milne, Drucilla. *The Amish of Harmony.* Harmony, MN: SMilne, 1993.

Overcott, Art. Posting to *MnBird@*linux2.Winona.msus.edu. 31 Oct. 1999.

Skutch, Alexander. *Parent Birds and Their Young.* Austin:

University of Texas, 1976.

The Holy Bible. I John 2:15-17, I Corinthians 5:11, Deuteronomy 5:8

van Braght, Thielman J. *The Martyrs' Mirror*. Netherlands, 1660.

Printed in the United States
849000003B